“*Immersed in Jesus Christ, T*
with the reality of God at w... the lives of people all over the world. Aretta Loving is a skillful communicator whose words will draw you into the place where you, too, can experience the Light of the World.”
—Robert Whitlow, best-selling author of *Water's Edge*

“Your interest in, prayers for, and involvement with, missions will increase dramatically as you read these amazing stories in *Immersed in Jesus Christ, The Light of the World* of how our Lord used ordinary people to do extra-ordinary things that changed lives and will continue to bring many into His kingdom.”
—Dr. Evelyn C. Davis, Training Consultant, SIL International

“I am honored to have my son's story in Aretta Loving's book. As you read *Immersed in Jesus Christ, The Light of the World*, you will feel you are standing in the presence of the Light Himself. And when we stand there, we realize how much He loves us!”
—Dr. John M. Perkins, JMP Foundation for Reconciliation and Development, Jackson, Mississippi

“Aretta Loving's page-turner stories show a supernatural God, active in the lives of His people. Readers are skillfully called to become *Immersed in Jesus Christ, The Light of the World* and to become more aware of Jesus Christ powerfully at work in our own lives.”
—Verna Kokmeyer, Maranatha Writers' Conference Director

“I highly recommend Aretta Loving's *Immersed in Jesus Christ, The Light of the World* to our Shiloh Church Fellowship and to all ARP churches. Her book will hold your interest, and it will challenge you to be more aware of the Light of the World and to live in His light.”
—Pastor Mark Miller, Shiloh, ARP, Lancaster, South Carolina

“Aretta Loving has done it again. Her third book is another ‘hard to lay down’ book. And as you read it and believe that miracles do happen, your life will be changed.”
—Marilyn Laszlo, Laszlo Mission League, former Bible translator in Papua New Guinea

“Aretta Loving's book will excite you as you read her stories from people who have seen a light miraculously or have met the Light!”
—Jim Jacob, Esq., author of *A Lawyer's Case for God*

"In *Immersed in Jesus Christ, The Light of the World,* Aretta captures your attention as she relates the miracle stories in the making. I have witnessed such miracles as a lay volunteer in mission overseas and in the US. '...He is able to do exceedingly abundantly above all we can ask or think' (Ephesians 3:20)."
—Bob Nelson, lay pastor and Bible study leader in the Rockfish Valley of the Blue Ridge Mountains, Virginia.

"Be encouraged in your walk with Jesus as you read Aretta Loving's latest book. Be challenged to trust God for everyday miracles as you study the lives of those who have followed His mandate to 'go into all the world and preach the Gospel.'"
—John Williams, JAARS Chaplain

"Aretta Loving has captured the very essence of missions. In her book she presents readers with several people whom God called to be missionaries. Each one of these servants of God is unique both in calling and personality. God calls a variety of people to do the Great Commission. If people are attentive to the Lord while reading this book, they may sense God's personal calling to missions as well."
—Dr. Donnie Gambel, pastor of Hermon Baptist Church, Waxhaw, North Carolina

"If we knew even a tenth of what God is doing in the world we would be utterly astonished. Aretta's stories help fill the gap between God building his church and our knowledge. I always enjoyed Ed and Aretta's presentations and now I applaud her newest book."
—Grace Fabian, author of *Outrageous Grace*, speaker, teacher

"We highly recommend Aretta Loving's *Immersed in Jesus Christ, The Light of the World* to all members of Lutheran Bible Translators (LBT). It will encourage and challenge them to be more aware of the Light of the World and to live in His light."
—Horst and Eugenie Schulz, members of LBT

Immersed in Jesus Christ
The Light of the World

Aretta Loving

Gazelle Press
Mobile, Alabama

Immersed in Jesus Christ, The Light of the World
by Aretta Loving

ISBN 978-1-58169-453-6
For Worldwide Distribution
Printed in the U.S.A.

Gazelle Press
P.O. Box 191540 • Mobile, AL 36619
800-367-8203

Contents

1 "That's the Man!" 1
2 A Radiant Little Boy 5
3 Religious, Rebelled, and Redeemed! 8
4 "Go West, Young Woman!" 14
5 Stay Away From This Man! 18
6 Another Man To Stay Away From! 22
7 An Angel With No Halo 29
8 A Broken Man 33
9 The Lovings Tell Their Story 41
10 What Brings Joy and Brightness Into a Life? 46
11 Double Exposure 49
12 "Washa Doin' Today, Tee-imm?" 54
13 Out of Witchcraft into the Light 58
14 Investment through Involvement 64
15 "Pray for My Wife!" 68
16 From Serving the Devil to Serving God in Bible Translation 71
17 The Woman That Cops Love to Hug! 76
18 "Counterfeit Brown Paper?" 80
19 "Just a Computer" 84
20 Encircled by a Halo 87
21 The Power of Blessing 91
22 "I Will Follow" 94
23 "Silent Night" United Common Enemies 99
24 A Most Inconvenient Christmas 105

25 "I Got Something Better'n a Big Buck This Year!" 109
26 "Handle With Care!" 111
27 Who Is This Jesus and This Power? 115
28 "Talk About Changed Lives!" 120
29 "The Light of God's Word Flooded My Soul!" 123
30 "Lord, I Need Help!" 129
31 Creativity and Faith—God's Gifts 134
32 Lost 137
33 "It Was As If God Had Removed My Eyes and Replaced Them with His" 146

Appendix A: Books on Light and Miracles 152
Appendix B: Resources on Salvation 152

Chapter 1

"That's the Man!"

Z. Tzorakye[1]

"In the last days, God says, I will pour out my Spirit on all people.... I will show wonders in the heaven above and signs on the earth below..." (Acts 2:17, 19).

A terrible flood occurred in a highly restricted area. The "JESUS" film teams, risking their lives, went out with boats to rescue as many people as possible. And once safe, they showed the people "JESUS."

In one of the flooded places, the water was steadily rising. One by one, everyone left, except one lone man. That man was a maker of suicide vests and bombs. His home was in the center of radical activity, a "workshop of death," filled with explosives of all kinds—wiring, vests, and detonators. He too wanted to leave. But then word came down from a top radical leader that he was to stay and protect the explosives, even at the cost of his life. He obeyed. So there he remained in the silence, alone behind his locked door, fearing he was about to drown.

Suddenly there was a loud and authoritative banging at the door. The man, feeling compelled to respond, unlatched and opened the door. Immediately the waters rushed in, swamping and ruining all his tools of death. But before him was an amazing sight—a man dressed in brilliant white. "Stop protecting these things that destroy. Follow Me," the man said. Thinking the man in white was a religious leader of a very high order, he obeyed and began walking with Him, hand in hand.

When he arrived on dry land where a group of people had gathered, all were amazed.

"How did you cross the flood?" they asked.

He explained how the man in brilliant white had led him out, and how they had crossed the flood by walking on the water. He could hardly believe what had just happened. It was like a dream to him.

Knowing that God had, indeed, just saved his life, film workers arranged to show him the "JESUS" film. When he saw Jesus as portrayed in the film, the bomb maker shouted out, "That's the man!"

Teams working in this difficult area now report that upwards of 50 percent of new believers came to faith after they experienced a vision, dream, or appearance of Jesus. When the workers hear them mention the "man in white," they show the film, and it's not uncommon that they respond in the same way: "That's the man!"

You may rightly ask, "Why does Jesus appear in this way?" and "Why visions?" Perhaps it's because the chains of spiritual darkness and oppression are so strong. Only Jesus can overpower demonic prisons of deception. Some have asked if we believe that the historic Jesus actually looked like the man chose to play Jesus in the film. No, but we do believe that the Holy Spirit causes this association in appearance, to verify the Truth to people who live in these oppressive areas.

It is a fact that the Risen Lord has appeared to many, many people, and the teams have often shown the film in response to an appearance. It is believed in one area, a center of terrorism, that there are now twenty thousand followers of Jesus as a result of people experiencing the "JESUS" film. In addition, sixty new believers are engaged in theological studies to lead newly formed churches or small groups. Many of them were once part of a well-known terrorist organization. When asked why they are risking so much, even death, they reply, "Because now we have found the Truth."

Some of these people have become members of a film team. In the process, a few have lost their lives for His name's sake. But the remainder persist so their friends, neighbors, and families might also be delivered from darkness. They surely identify with the apostle Paul, who wrote:

> "*We are hard pressed on every side, but not crushed; perplexed, but not in despair; persecuted, but not abandoned; struck down, but not destroyed. We always carry around in our body the death of Jesus, so that the life of Jesus may also be revealed in our body*" (2 Corinthians 4:8–12).

Yes, it is happening as the old song says it would:
All over the world the Spirit is moving,
All over the world, as the prophet said it would be,
All over the world there's a mighty revelation
Of the glory of the Lord, as the waters cover the sea.

More about The "JESUS" Film Project:

The Project distributes the film *Jesus*, a two-hour docudrama of the life of Christ based on the Gospel of Luke. The goal of the "JESUS" Film Project is to reach every nation, tribe, people, and tongue, helping them see and hear the story of Jesus in a language they can understand. So whether a people speaks Swahili, French, or a language whose name is extremely difficult to pronounce, they will encounter the life and message of Jesus in their own heart language. The film has been seen in every country of the world and translated into hundreds of languages since its initial release in 1979.

Many mission experts have acclaimed the *Jesus* film as one of the greatest evangelistic success stories of all time. The ultimate success of this project won't be measured by how many people have seen it, but by how many follow Him after seeing this film.

Through use by the "JESUS" Film Project and more than 1,500 Christian agencies, this powerful film has had more than six billion viewings worldwide since 1979. As a result, more than 200 million people have indicated decisions to accept Christ as Savior and Lord!

1 For security purposes Tzorakye, a pseudonym, is used.

Chapter 2

A Radiant Little Boy

Spencer Perkins

> Radiance can be seen in the faces of those who have experienced Jesus Christ's Divine Radiance. —*Anonymous*

"Daddy, will you come to church with me so I can win a prize?" four-year-old Spencer asked his father.

Spencer's request only caused negative feelings to surface in his father. He loved his son, but… "My background had prejudiced me against the church, especially the black church," his father says. "My family had rejected the church, looking on it as a tool to make a person weak and dependent—just one more kind of exploitation of black people. And I couldn't even imagine someone called a 'white Christian.' I looked on the white church as a private club of oppressors, and it had nothing to do with reality and justice."

"Then in 1957, in a quiet way, God began to show me the unimaginable," he says. "My wife, Vera Mae, enrolled Spencer in a children's Bible class at a little church down the street. He'd come home real happy. In those days we just sat down and ate our meals. But Spencer wanted to pray and say Bible verses before we ate."

And Spencer kept after his father to "come to church with me, Daddy!"

"Something was happening to Spencer—something I knew nothing about. I'd never before seen Christianity at work like that in anyone's life. At work in a beautiful way. Because I loved my son, I finally went with him. Besides, I wanted to find out what they taught to make Spencer such a radiant little boy."

And John found that they were simply teaching the Bible! In 1998 Spencer had a heart attack. When he left and went to be with his Lord, he left "a radiance, a shining peace." And we can only imagine the radiance that surrounded him as he stood before the Lord of Radiance.

***More about Spencer Perkins*:**

Spencer and Chris Rice wrote *Racial Healing for the Sake of the Gospel: More Than Equals.* After growing up in two different worlds, Spencer and Chris were brought together by God to become friends and partners for more than a decade in the difficult ministry of racial reconciliation. From their experience they offer hope that whites and African Americans can live together in peace. More than ever, this book shows how the cause of racial reconciliation needs yokefellows for the sake of racial harmony and the witness of the gospel and is a recipient of a *Christianity Today* 1994 Critics Choice Award. Here is *living proof* that white and black Christians can live together.

When Spencer Perkins was sixteen years old, he visited his bloodied and swollen father (Pastor John Perkins) in jail. Police had beaten the black activist severely, and Spencer never forgot the moment. He couldn't imagine living in community with a white person after that. But his plans were changed. Chris Rice grew up in very different circumstances. He was of "Vermont Yankee stock," attending an elite Eastern college and looking forward to a career in law and government. But his plans were also changed. Spencer and Chris became not only friends but yokefellows and partners for more than a decade in the difficult ministry of racial reconciliation. From their own hard-won experience, they show that there is hope for our frightening race problem, that whites and African Americans can live together in peace. "The cause of racial reconciliation needs yokefellows," they argue, "...not solely for the sake of racial harmony—even though it will lead to that—but for the witness of the gospel."

After the death of his son in 1998, Dr. John Perkins returned to Mississippi and bought the property once owned by Spencer and his Antioch Community. There he established the Spencer Perkins Center, the youth arm of the John M. Perkins Foundation. The Foundation has developed youth programs such as After School Tutorial, Summer Arts Camp, Junior and College Internship Program, Good News Bible Club, Young Life, and Jubilee Youth Garden. The Foundation also has a housing arm, "Zechariah 8," that provides affordable housing for low- to moderate-income families with a focus on single mothers.

Chapter 3

Religious, Rebelled, and Redeemed!

Sam Nadler

Consider living plants. All grow because of the sun,
but they also grow toward the sun.
The light determines not only the *fact* of growth
but also the *direction* of growth.
In this natural realm plants "seek" greater exposure
to those life-giving rays.

Mercy received reorients the soul not only *into* the Light
but also *toward* the Light of Christ.
In nature some trees serve to block the necessary sunlight
and thereby stunt growth in others.
Yet that's never the case in the Lord.

Those who've grown more in admiring Christ, in focusing on His Person, in desiring Him, in delighting in Him, and in loving the heavenly Man over all the earth, over all else, and over self, these people don't block the Light but reflect the Light and enable more growth.

—Bill Powell, *Daily Devotional from the Beatitudes of Jesus*

Sam was born on a snowy winter day in early January 1948 in Queens, New York. Growing up there in that neighborhood middle village in the late forties and early fifties meant growing up Jewish. It also meant that people who had gone through the Holocaust lived there. When ten years old, Sam went to a rabbi with a question that he often asked himself: *Where was God when this was going on?*

The rabbi's answer did nothing to satisfy Sam: "I tell myself, *He who believes does not question. And he who questions does not believe.*"

Religious

With a synagogue on every block, the choices of where to attend seemed endless. But as Sam says, "Where my family attended depended mostly on who we were getting along with during any given High Holy Day season."

Sam continues, "I received a normal Jewish upbringing and was eventually Bar Mitzvahed according to orthodoxy. That both pleased and relieved my family, because even at such a young age I tended to resist religion.

"I had questions. A number of Auschwitz survivors in our neighborhood had numbers on their arms. Those numbers were a constant argument for me against God's existence. *How could there be a God, much less a 'God of Israel,' who would allow such atrocities to be perpetrated against people, especially the Jewish people?*"

One night when Sam was nine years old, he put God to the test: "Okay, if You're there, have a penny appear under my pillow," he demanded. "I figured I wasn't greedy—anyone can come up with a penny, right? So the next morning when there was no penny under my pillow, I concluded there was no God over my head either."

After his Bar Mitzvah, the pressure lifted for him to attend synagogue. "My parents no longer felt responsible for my spiritual commitments or failures as they now considered me an adult. So I gave up any participation in religion, which I'd only done to honor my family."

Rebelled

"I spent my teenage years removing any residual effects of religiosity. I actually took great pride in talking my friends out of going to services, whether church or synagogue. I got involved in local crime, and the police would occasionally show up at the door, raising suspicions among our neighbors. And so I became, I'm now sorry to say, a source of disappointment to my family.

"Following my stint in Vietnam, where I developed a fondness for selling drugs, I lived in various scenic locales of California. At first I traveled around and lived in an old green Econoline van that I called 'Wire and Whimsy,' because that was what held it together. It was sort of a 'rolling party,' even though an elderly van requires one to be more of a mechanic than a poet. I broke down in Eureka, California, and got a job there at Snug Saloon—a bar for hippies, fishermen, and lumberjacks. Customers were not only provided entertainment in the form of nightly brawls, but the place also gave me somewhere to crash until the van was fixed.

"It was there that I met my first Christians—genuine believers in Messiah. Around closing time, they would come in to give the drunks a place to sleep, which was fine with me, since I had to do something with them anyway.

"But these were troublemaking Christians: they would take the opportunity to talk about Jesus to whoever was still on their feet! It turns out that talking about Jesus in a saloon is really bad for business, so I'd throw out those zealots, with or without the drunks. Nothing personal, but business is business.

"One night one of those Christians tried to tell me how much I needed the Lord. 'You'll never be truly happy until you come to faith in Jesus,' she said."

Sam wanted to show her how "happy" he really was, so he laughed at her, then said, "I have so much religion of my own that I'm not even using, what would I want with any of yours?" He went on to say what he calls some "rather creative and colorful, but not very flattering things."

But that night something happened to him. "I was not aware of it then, but a spiritual seed was planted. Circumstances changed very quickly after that. The saloon changed hands, the house I was living in burned down, but the van was still running somewhat, so I figured it was time to move on.

"Back in San Francisco I shared a flat with about a dozen other 'denizens of the dark'—all involved in one illegal activity or another, generally drug-oriented. It was during that time that I met a Jew who believed in Jesus. He was witnessing to some people where I did business—sort of a place 'where angels fear to tread.' When he told me he was Jewish, I genuinely felt sorry for him. I figured his mother must have dressed him wrong growing up or something. This had to be the dumbest Jew I ever met, for if there's one thing a Jew should know, it is that *Jews do not believe in Jesus. Period.*"

He invited Sam to a Bible study, but Sam mocked him. "Thursday night? Sorry, that's my night to sleep in, but if I come down with insomnia, I'll be sure to drop by.

"And the strange thing is, the night of that study I decided on a whim to go, just to laugh at the believers. While I was there, someone showed me a portion from the Hebrew Prophets: Isaiah 53. I read it. I couldn't believe my eyes. It spoke of One who would die for the sins of my people but not stay dead! Nothing is supposed to be that clear, especially not the Bible! You see, I considered spiritual matters were supposed to be vague, and you could interpret what it meant for you. There isn't supposed to be objective evidence. These sneaky Christians, acting so sincere and Jewish—they must have taken part of their New Testament and stuck it in my side of the Bible. They were confusing me with the facts! I pretended not to be interested. When they said they would pray for me and wrote my name in their Bibles, I could only sarcastically laugh and go back to the little world I was familiar with and comfortable in.

"Things began to change, though. Over the next several months, the more I tried to disprove what they were saying, the more intrigued I became with Jesus. I even tried studying the occult, and what is now called 'New Age' religion. I took courses at the Metaphysical Institute of San Francisco. But the more I searched for truth in all the wrong places, the more I came back to considering Jesus."

Redeemed!

"On the evening of January 10, 1972, I became convinced of the spiritual reality of evil. Until then I had figured there was no objective right and wrong: spiritual power to me was simply what you made of it. It was then that I realized that drugs were opening me up to the spiritual realm—but to the wrong spirits! I saw a spiritual battle for my soul, a battle I was losing, and I was thoroughly convinced that I needed a Savior. I needed Jesus.

"Though I didn't know all the right words to say, I asked Jesus to save me. And He did. When I prayed that simple prayer, the Spirit of God came down upon me with power. I was cleansed, forgiven, and I experienced a peace I had never known before: a peace that passes all understanding.

"I awoke the next morning and I knew in my heart one thing: *Jesus is Lord.* I don't know how I knew that, but I did. I also knew I could not live where I was living or the way I was living, but what was I to do? I thought surely I had to be the only real Jew who had ever done this before. After a few dead ends, I remembered the Bible study I had attended months before. *Maybe they know what to do,* I thought.

"I called someone from the Bible study, feeling sure no one would remember me, so I explained who I was. I finally blurted out, 'Jesus saved me last night—what do I do now?'

"The other end of the line sounded like the 'Hallelujah Chorus'! They hadn't forgotten me. They had been praying for me *every day*. Even though I hadn't believed in prayer, they believed that there is a God who answers prayer. So if you're praying for someone, don't stop. The Lord *does* answer prayer!

"I soon started studying the Scriptures, growing in Messiah and learning to share Him with others. There were many more blessings to follow. I went off to Bible college, and soon after, I met and married Miriam. The Lord called me to being the good news to my people—something I've attempted to do for the past thirty-plus years. Some of that will have to wait to be told at another time, but this is my story, and I'm sticking to it!"

More about Sam Nadler:

Sam is the leader of the Word of Messiah Ministries in Charlotte, North Carolina where he and his family reside.

A brochure called "Sam's Story: A Jewish Testimony of Faith in Messiah: Religious, Rebellious, and Redeemed" provided the basis of Sam's story. Most of what is written here is exactly as he wrote it, though in a few places, with his permission, I have changed first person to third person and taken some minor liberties to shorten or rearrange sentences. The brochure ends with these words: "If you want to know more about the Messiah, please contact us at:

SAM NADLER
WORD OF MESSIAH MINISTRIES
P.O. BOX 79238
CHARLOTTE, NC 28271
PHONE/FAX: 704-544-1948
WWW.WORDOFMESSIAH.ORG"

Chapter 4

"Go West, Young Woman!"

Miriam Nadler

Darkness cannot drive out darkness; only light can do that.
Hate cannot drive out hate; only love can do that.
—*Martin Luther King Jr.*

During Miriam's college years as a very young believer, she was discipled by Arnold Fruchtenbaum, a Jewish man who believed in Jesus. Today, Fruchtenbaum leads Ariel Ministries.[1]

"Even though I was basically immature and untaught in the Scriptures," Marian says, "for some reason Arnold saw in me ministry potential. As he discipled me in aspects of the faith—such as believing God to provide for my school expenses as I worked my way through college—he also gave me an understanding and a love for the Jewish people. For my English and history papers, he encouraged me to write on various aspects of Jewish life, especially the Holocaust."

Miriam became involved in a prayer group that Fruchtenbaum led for Israel. There the Lord gave Miriam an even deeper love for the Jewish people and put a burden on her heart to reach out to them.

After graduating from Cedarville University with a degree in teaching, Miriam had a certainty that God was calling her to minister to Jewish people. But before she could begin that ministry, she first had to teach for a short while to pay off her college bills. "That done, I moved to New York City with great joy and anticipation," she says "because I knew the Lord was leading me to work with Chosen People Ministries."[2]

During her first six months in the city, she studied under Moshe Rosen, who later started Jews for Jesus.[3] She immersed herself in Jewish culture, learning the Hebrew language and Israeli music. She began a Bible study for Jewish women that met every Friday night. "I often cooked a meal, and about a dozen women would gather to eat," Miriam says. "Then I would teach and disciple them in God's Word."

After three years of ministry in New York City, Miriam had the opportunity to go to Israel. There she studied at the University of Jerusalem and took some graduate courses. She also studied Hebrew at an *ulpan*—an institute or school for the intensive study of Hebrew. Not only did she study there, but she also had a ministry there. Through one-on-one friendships and a coffeehouse that she helped establish, she had the opportunity to share her faith. After a year in Israel she moved back to New York City for a while, then God led her to move out west to California. There she helped start Jews for Jesus.

"When we began a music team called the Liberated Wailing Wall, I met a new believer named Sam Nadler. The Lord definitely brought us together in love and ministry. For the first few years of our married lives, we were on the road, crisscrossing the USA, doing concerts for evangelistic outreach."

Eventually the Nadlers' touring days ended, and they moved to New York City. There they began their outreach ministry by opening the New York branch of Jews for Jesus. Miriam discipled women one-on-one and in small groups.

God called Sam to provide leadership for Chosen People

Ministries between 1979 and 1996. Miriam worked alongside him as they planted Messianic congregations. In 1997 they began Word of Messiah Ministries in order to build up congregations through practical discipleship materials.

Today Miriam serves her Savior by leading the women's ministries at Hope of Israel Congregation in Charlotte, North Carolina—Word of Messiah Ministries.

***More about Miriam Nadler*:**

Miriam has been in active ministry for thirty-eight years, discipling and teaching women. She presently serves with Word of Messiah Ministries in Charlotte, North Carolina. As a gifted teacher, she travels throughout the US, Europe, and Israel. Miriam and her husband, Sam, have two grown sons, Joshua and Matthew. Joshua lives in Los Angeles and works for Sony Pictures, finding and editing family-friendly films, and Matthew lives in Charlotte and serves as director of publication for Word of Messiah Ministries. Phone/Fax: 704-544-1948; www.wordofmessiah.org

1 *Ariel Ministries*, established by Arnold Fruchtenbaum, seeks to evangelize and disciple Jewish people. *Ariel* means "lion of God," representing the Messiah, *Yeshua*, as the Lion of Judah. It is also an alternate name for Jerusalem (see Isaiah 29:1). In 1966, a burning seed of desire was planted in the heart of Arnold Fruchtenbaum to work with his Jewish people when he was in Jerusalem. In 1971 he graduated from Dallas Theological Seminary, and then he and his wife, Mary Ann, moved to Israel. There they established a Bible institute, which became so effective in discipleship that after two years, religious leaders forced them to return to the United States. When they returned, they saw the Holy Spirit doing a work among Jewish young people, with an explosion of new believers rivaling that recorded in the Book of Acts. But along with the joy of seeing hundreds saved came the agony of watching new Jewish believers falter and ebb in their enthusiasm.

The concept of a new ministry simmered within Fruchtenbaum's heart during the following years, as he worked with the American Board of Missions to the Jews (now Chosen People Ministries), and later, The Christian Jew Foundation. Ariel Ministries was born in San Antonio, Texas, in late 1977. In 1989, Fruchtenbaum received an Ph.D. from New York University.

2 *Chosen People Ministries* was founded in Brooklyn, New York, in 1894 by Rabbi Leopold Cohn, a Hungarian Jewish immigrant with a zeal to share the knowledge of *Yeshua*, the Messiah, with God's chosen people. The mission exists to pray for, evangelize, disciple, and serve Jewish people everywhere and also to help fellow believers do the same. Today, Chosen People Ministries serves in thirteen countries. Its outreach programs include evangelism and discipleship, Messianic Centers and congregations, equipping the local church for Jewish evangelism, print and web publications, and benevolence toward Jewish people.

3 *Jews for Jesus* was founded by Martin "Moishe" Rosen in 1973. Rosen's mission, having converted to Christianity himself, was to help bring other Jews to the Christian faith. He became a Baptist minister and a member of the American Board of Missions to the Jews (ABMJ). The ABMJ's goal was to convert Jews. Rosen soon realized that most Jewish people were unwilling to leave their Jewish traditions behind. Therefore Rosen left the ABMJ and started Jews for Jesus, an organization aimed at converting Jews while allowing them to keep their religious practices.

Chapter 5

Stay Away From This Man!

Dean Jordan

Jesus came to them and said, "All authority in heaven and on earth has been given to me. Therefore go and make disciples of all nations, baptizing them in the name of the Father and of the Son and of the Holy Spirit, and teaching them to obey everything I have commanded you. And surely I am with you always, to the very end of the age" (Matthew 28:18–20).

Dean is my coworker at the JAARS Center.[1] And I recommend that some people stay away from him—those who don't want to hear about Jesus.

Dean's face shines with the light of Jesus. And he takes—or more often, he makes—opportunities to tell just about every person he meets about Jesus.

Dean's method of telling people about Jesus: When not in Africa working with national people to translate the Old Testament, Dean and others of like spirit spend time each Saturday at a local flea market. There they pass out million and trillion dollar bills! Well, not real million or trillion dollar bills, but ones with a gospel message on them. He says he purchases these from Livingwaters.com, phone number 1-800-437-1893, and that they are not copyrighted, so you can print out your own copies.) As he walks around, he notes that "Seldom do people refuse and often they will ask for more of the bills to share with friends or family members."

Once a person has accepted the bill, he stops to talk with those who show an interest in talking. "This is worth more than a million dollars," he tells the person, " but you have to read what is on the back to know why. After all, will a million dollars buy your way into heaven?"

If they find the print too small to read or they indicate a further interest, he gives them a 5½ by 8½ pamphlet titled "Good Person Survey."[2] This four-page pamphlet invites the person to "Take the survey!" After going through four of the Ten Commandments, people find out they have fallen short of God's standard and are destined for a place they don't want to go to. On the back page is the good news: "God doesn't want us to go there either and He sent His Son Jesus to pay our fine."

"The Good Person Survey continues to grow in use and distribution," Dean reports. "Over 12,000 are in print in English, Spanish, and Nafaanra, and it will soon be in Korean and German.

"And almost daily, exciting things happen when I share these. Three recent examples –

- The 4th of July means a celebration parade, and I take advantage of these. Yesterday I left our Waxhaw parade praising and celebrating a new birth! Last year at the parade, I met the young man who I had given a "Good Person Survey" last year. At that point in his life, he hadn't seriously considered a relationship with God. But when I talked to him yesterday, I rejoiced as I saw that his attitude and life had drastically changed since last year!
- The last time when in Ghana waiting for a Ghanaian coworker to finish shopping in the market, I gave a "Good Person Survey" to a young lady selling plantain chips. She

immediately began to read it aloud to a crowd of about twenty-five people.

- Then the day I was to leave Ghana to start my long trip back to the US, one of the Ghanaian translators with me announced that the Paramount Chief of all the Nafana people was in town. "We must go to the palace and pay our respects," he said. So I finished packing and went by the Chief's house. While there I shared the "Good Person Survey" with him and a group of elders there with him. They were discussing it among themselves and seemed to receive it very well. I may not know the results of that until eternity, but I believe I'll rejoice when I hear those results!

Recently Dean stopped at the Waxhaw post office where "I just wanted to buy a few stamps," he says. "The line was long and some had several packages to mail so I had time to pass out a few million-dollar bills. The guy in front of me was a grumpy ol' one. That kinda discouraged me, and I didn't think anything was going to go anywhere. There were two windows where mail was being given out. The woman in the third window was just getting people's mail out of their boxes. She asked if there were any more people in line just to get their mail. Everyone in line said no. I asked her if she'd be willing to give me some stamps since that was all I wanted and was told no.

"A lady in front of me said, 'Come on up and get in front of me, if all you want is stamps.'

"'Are you sure?' I asked her.

"'Yes, come on!' she replied.

"I went up and told the lady, 'I appreciate what you did. You've saved me a lot of time. Now I'd like to show my appreciation by giving both you and your friend a million-dollar bill.'

"They got excited as they read them. 'Hey! This is great!'

"I looked at the people behind us and asked, 'Would any of you like one, too?'

"Everyone, even the grumpy one, said yes! Right before my eyes, I saw the Lord put a situation together that just didn't seem like it was going to work!

"All of this is the fulfillment of my life's Scripture verse– *But thanks be to God who in Christ always leads us in triumph, and through us spreads the fragrance of the knowledge of Him everywhere* (2 Cor. 2:14 RSV). I believe this is disciple making and what God called each of us to do."

More about Dean Jordan:

Since the early 1970s, Dean and his wife, Carol, have served with Wycliffe Bible Translators. Working with the Nafana people in Ghana, they translated the Nafaanra New Testament.

They now live in Waxhaw, North Carolina, near JAARS, Wycliffe's support center, to be able to care for Carol's elderly mother. They have one daughter and four grandchildren—one of whom is with the Lord.

Dean makes trips to Ghana a couple of times a year to help a community-appointed committee of Nafana people with the translation of the Nafaanra Old Testament.

"The exciting translation news," Deans says, "is that the Nafaanra team has now prepared the New Testament, which has been sold out for about five years, for reprinting. We hope to finish checking the Nafaanra Old Testament and have the whole Nafaanra Bible ready for printing soon.

"We are excited to be on the home stretch. But pray! Satan is not happy to see this happen, as his goal is to steal, kill, and destroy."

1 The Jaars Center, Wycliffe's support center, is located in Waxhaw, North Carolina.

2 See Appendix B.

Chapter 6

Another Man To Stay Away From!

Tom Hodges

Always be prepared to give an answer to everyone who asks you… (1 Peter 3:15).

When Tom quotes 1 Peter 3:15 to an audience, he always says, "And if they don't ask, find a way to tell them anyway, since we're told in Matthew 28:18–20 to *go and preach the gospel.*" And if you're not a preacher, Colossians 3:16 in *The Living Bible* admonishes us to *Remember what Christ taught and let his words enrich your lives and make you wise; teach them to each other....*

And Tom adds, "Yes, and we are not only to be prepared to give an answer for the hope we have in Jesus, but we are to do this with 'gentleness and respect,' as Peter adds. Even if that one is a scruffy, long-haired hippie."

In Yugoslavia, Tom had opportunity to do this. As Tom talked to him, the young hippie listened attentively with a smirk on his face. Once Tom finished, without comment, the young man took out his cigarette lighter and set the tract on fire!

"Thank you for demonstrating the end result of rejecting Christ," Tom said. Then he turned and walked away, praying that his last words would sink into the young man's heart as he stood with the burning tract in his hand.

Tom says he specializes in "casual witnessing to *targets of opportunity*." Most recently his "targets of opportunity" have included several new neighbors he met at their mailbox out on the street or those who pass by his house—for instance, a teenage boy on his bicycle who stopped to watch him cut the grass and heard about how he could become a Christian home repairman. And the list goes on.

A FedEx man brought a package to the Hodges's house and ended up getting "the package of eternal life." Yes, the Holy Spirit had prepared that man's heart! He prayed to receive Christ while standing by his truck in front of the Hodges's house.

Not all are receptive. Recently Tom shared a one-minute version of how he came to Christ and gave a tract—"Is the Bible True?"—to a woman.

"If looks could kill, I'd be dead now!" he says. "I wondered if she had lost a loved one recently and was reacting angrily against God, as some people do at such a time."

Tom's methods of witness to "targets":

Casual Witnessing

How does he begin his casual witnessing after opening any conversation? Like the Gadarene, Tom does it by telling what great things God has done for him. He says that this usually captures people's attention "since so many people are living empty, unfulfilled lives without Christ—as I was. If it were not for Jesus, I would've been a drunk like most of my uncles. I eventually found life so empty I was headed for suicide. I was formerly an atheistic radar field engineer assigned to a navy fighter squadron. And in spite of having won a letter of commendation from the U.S. Naval Bureau of Weapons for my work with air-to-air missiles, my heart was empty and life pointless."

Then he continues to tell them about his atheistic life and his Jeremiah 29:13[1] search for meaning in world religions and drink, which ended in total despair. He tells them how as an atheist he found God, at first superficially through scientific evidence, then truly believing by seeing himself as a sinner needing God's forgiveness. He shares how today his life is full of joy and meaningful activities.

The conversation turns next to where they stand. Tom reads them some Scripture portions and then talks about the consequences of living a life without Christ. An invitation is given, asking if they wish to continue the conversation. The objective is to either strengthen their faith to also witness or invite them to receive Christ. "The door is always left open to contact me for inquiries. Not all witnessing goes all the way to the end for everyone, but I try. My basic progressive witnessing types, depending on their response and the situation, are 'Hit-'n'-Run,' 'Tract & Testimony' (one- or two-minute version), and 'Shoot the Works!'"

Eavesdrop Witnessing

"This may sound contrived, and if so, it's because it is," Tom says. In a public place, a friend asks Tom, "How did you become a believer?" and Tom, in turn, asks that friend the same question.

Captive Audience Witnessing

These conversations, which take place in medical waiting rooms, or on buses, trains, or planes, are a delight to Tom. He says that witnessing in medical waiting rooms is perhaps his most frequent witnessing activity.

Sometimes a captive audience can be arranged. Recently at a large mall Tom bought an item too heavy to carry a quarter mile to his car. Zack was assigned to take the package to a side door and wait there while Tom and his wife, Irene, brought the car around. However, Tom chose to remain behind—and he had plenty of time to talk to Zack about Christ.

He began the conversation by talking about the weather. "Yeah," Zack said, "and I have terrible allergies."

Tom then picked up on the marvel of pollen in fertilizing plants. "I never cared much about the marvels of nature when I was an atheist, but…." And from there he went right into how he became a believer and talked to Zack about his spiritual condition.

Tom says, "If you are prepared, you can turn most any conversation into an opportunity to talk about Christ. Many people will never go to church, but when they hear about Jesus from us in the everyday world, it can impact their lives for eternity."

Hat-Wearing Witnessing

On shopping trips Tom often wears his JAARS hat and some ask, "What is JAARS?"[2] Also, wearing his U.S.S. Ranger hat gives him opportunity for talking about Jesus. "I too served on the Ranger," or "Thank you so much for your service!" someone will say. And from there Tom begins to talk….

"That hat," Tom says, "also gets me a free meal at two restaurants on Veterans Day. Waiting areas are filled with other vets, a great place for opening a conversation!"

Five-Point Plan Tract

Tom always carries several types of tracts with his church stamp on them. His mission's Five-Point Plan is a staple since it's short and clear.[3] Over many decades the Holy Spirit has brought scores of prepared people to Christ using this tract. As a former atheist, apologetics is one of Tom's hobbies.

Depending on how open a person is, Tom will interject more on how he came to Christ by sharing, "Finally in desperation I confessed to God that I didn't know if He was real. 'If You are real, show me,' I prayed. And I told Him if He showed me He was real, I'd follow Him no matter what. But I also confessed I was unwilling to give up my sins and independence, so I asked God to make me willing. It took a while, but He did. Knowing I needed a wife, on my very first visit to a church in years with a big notebook of questions—mostly about 'Why does God…?'—God sent my future wife to get my attention by nearly running over me in the parking lot."

Tom's favorite door-to-door approach, which he's used for years, is his mission's Five-Point Plan. "I like it because it's short and clear. It begins with: Here's a few verses from the Bible that show how much God loves you. Do you ever read the Bible?"

If the person says yes: "Have you found the key verse that explains why the Bible was written? It's the first verse on the tract—John 20:31." And the person is asked to read it aloud.

If the person says no: "Then you've never found the 'key verse' that explains why it was written. It's the first verse on the tract—John 20:31." And the person is asked to read it aloud.

Following that are four more verses, ending with an invitation to receive Christ. In between each verse is a transition leading into the next verse. While the person is reading a verse, someone new at witnessing reviews the transition part. Then when the person finishes reading a verse, the witness shares the transition in his own words. He then invites the person to read the next verse, while he looks ahead for the next transition…and so on.

"It's a great way to train people to witness and can be done in an hour's time. I've seen strangers, who the Holy Spirit for years had been preparing, drop like ripe fruit into your hand. Tony was one such 'ripe fruit.' He later became a deacon in our church in England. Others need multiple visits to answer their questions and deal with their hang-ups. Number-wise, many will reject the gospel, but it's our job to just tell them.

"We used this technique going back to 1965 followed by years on three mission fields where it worked just as well. God prepares strangers in advance. Our job is just to reap what's ripe or help ripen what's there. It's amazing how the Holy Spirit can capture total strangers once they read a verse for themselves off the tract. Our mission has planted dozens of churches around the world using the Five-Point Plan in many languages."

While Tom may not share the gospel with every person he meets, he feels all true Christians are appointed as some type of ambassador with a ministry of reconciliation, just as it says in 2 Corinthians 5:14–21. Tom says, "Your testimony may not be a spectacular one. Perhaps you were in a church for years but did not know Jesus. Then one day you met Him and were born again. By bringing the Word to light, we can make the living Word—Jesus—come alive[4] for those who may never go to a church!"

More about Tom Hodges:

Tom and Irene are in their forty-sixth year as missionaries with Christians in Action Missions, International (CinA).

After the Hodges married, their witnessing led to a missionary call. They served in Italy for seven years, then another seven years in Britain where Tom trained missionaries and Irene worked in accounting. After those fourteen years, they returned to work at CinA. Bob Weber, a Bible translator, visited their church, and Tom learned that computers could drastically speed Bible translation. He was hooked, but it wasn't until 1998—twelve years later—that CinA could release them. At JAARS, Tom has served as a research assistant, programmer, and development tester over a ten-plus year period. He then worked at home on an enhancement for a speech analyzer used by Bible translators. And Irene has keyboarded over fifty Bible manuscripts or portions for Wycliffe Associates, UK, since 1999. "It's like eating ice cream and being paid to eat it, though our 'partners' actually support our ministry here at JAARS!" she says.

The Hodges have been blessed with a daughter and son—and a daughter-in-law for twenty-seven years—and two grandchildren.

Tom is currently writing a book with a working title of: *An Atheists Journey, Tom's Conversion from an Atheist Along with Answers to Common Questions by Skeptics.*

1 *You will seek me and find me when you seek me with all your heart* (Jeremiah 29:13).

2 The JAARS Center, Wycliffe's support center, is located in Waxhaw, North Carolina.

3 See Appendix B for the pamphlet.

4 *Paul, a servant of God and an apostle of Jesus Christ for the faith of God's elect and the knowledge of the truth that leads to godliness—a faith and knowledge resting on the hope of eternal life, which God, who does not lie, promised before the beginning of time, and at his appointed season he brought his word to light through the preaching entrusted to me by the command of God our Savior…* (Titus 1:1–3).

Chapter 7

An Angel With No Halo

Evie Lindquist

The Holy Spirit, in bodily form, descended on him like a dove (Luke 3:22 NLT).

Evie was tired and so very ready to get home to Lareau. Her speaking at the women's retreat had gone well. Her flight to the Ukraine also went well with no hitches. But now the retreat was over and… "I found myself becoming very weary with the drab and run-down conditions of my environment; I was physically tired and mentally exhausted. I was very anxious to be on my way home," Evie says.

The day finally came! She would be leaving Odessa to return home. To make sure she didn't miss her flight, she asked her host to take her to the airport early, and he graciously agreed to do so.

"I arrived at the airport over three hours early, and I was the only passenger in the room," Evie says. She describes the airport as "very unfriendly. It had not been kept up; in fact it looked as though it had been struck in World War II and never repaired."

A few men and some stray dogs and cats wandered in and out of the room where Evie sat. "I was very visible to those men, of course. I noticed that they would talk to one another while looking my way. There was a row of chairs, so I sat down on one and tried to read a book. After a while, I looked up to see a very unusual dog walk in. He had a collar around his neck, and was clean and healthy looking. He walked over to me, looked up into my face, sniffed me a couple of times, then jumped up onto the chair next to me. He sat there quietly, occasionally looking at me, as if to say *I'm still watching over you.*"

A few minutes passed—though to Evie it seemed more like an hour—and it was necessary for her to begin the boarding procedure. She gathered up her things, bid good-bye to "her dog," and left for the departure area, a large room with glass doors where she could look out and see the plane she would soon board.

"After a few minutes in the passenger room, I was surprised to see 'my dog' again! He came over to me and stayed at my side, then accompanied me to the bottom of the stairway to the aircraft. I told him good-bye and went to out to board the plane. As soon as I reached my seat, I looked out of the window, thinking I'd see my dog standing there wagging his tail. And I wanted to wave good-bye to him. But he was nowhere in sight. I suddenly realized I had been watched over by an angel—not only an unusual one, but one with no halo!"[1]

More about Evie Lindquist:

Evie married Laureau in August 1961. In the early spring of 1986, Lareau and Evie Lindquist accepted a two-week assignment with Wycliffe Bible Translators in Colombia, South America. They were unexpectedly detained in a remote area of the jungle, Cona Colorado. During the evening and late into the night as they were walking the small airstrip, the concept of Barnabas was born. They had had many opportunities for service over their years together, but the Lord was moving in their hearts to consider a ministry of encouragement to God's servants. After much prayer, Barnabas International became a reality on July 7, 1986.

Barnabas International focuses on providing encouragement and member care to MKs; missionaries—whether at home or abroad; pastors; and national church leaders. They serve as pastoral care providers, shepherding the hearts and souls of God's people and their families. Executive Perry Branford writes, "We provide encouragement to God's global servants through:

Going: We travel to the fields of service to provide an onsite ministry of presence.

Listening: We ask questions, taking time to listen to the servant's story.

Speaking: We minister the Word of God through preaching and teaching.

"Our intended audience moves beyond the growing number of specialists who are called 'Pastors to Missionaries' to include all who care for missionaries. Those pastors we minister to include ordained or lay pastoral care providers, who may serve in this ministry as a secondary task. The common denominator that brings us together is a desire to care for the hearts and souls of those who live out the Great Commission cross-culturally."

Lareau has recently published *Glory, Glory, Glory: Focusing on the Glory of God* with Xulon Press. He was motivated by 1 Corinthians 10:31, which reads: *So whether you eat or drink or whatever you do, do it all for the glory of God.*

You may contact Lareau and Evie Lindquist directly at 815-395-1335 or by e-mail at barnabas@barnabas.org.

1 God the Holy Spirit was willing to appear as a dove and light on Jesus after His baptism. An angel is pure spirit, and as such, has no shape. There is no reason an angel could not appear even in *animal* form. For the purpose of interacting with us, an angel may at times assume a shape in order to fulfill the purpose God intends for the angel to accomplish. If for the purpose of the angel's visit to be accomplished the angel wants to

be recognized, the angel would most likely assume a shape that would allow this. But the purpose of an angel's visit may require an angel to go unrecognized. The author of Hebrews admonishes Christians: *Do not forget to entertain strangers, for by so doing some people have entertained angels without knowing it* (Hebrews 13:2).

Chapter 8

A Broken Man

William Harness

> At times our own light goes out and is rekindled by a spark from another person. Each of us has cause to think with deep gratitude of those who have lighted the flame within us.
> —*Albert Schweitzer*

"I need to talk..." a broken man confessed to a friend one evening. Their talk ran into the early hours of the morning as his friend listened to and prayed for him. "I cried as I told him of God's call on my life. I confessed that I'd not only blown that call, but I'd also blown my testimony and my relationship with my wife and children. That was in 1977. That broken man's marriage and his relationship with his children was—by God's grace—restored! I know because I am that broken man," says Bill Harness.

Today as Bill sings "I'd rather have Jesus than anything... than to be a king of a vast domain..." in concerts across the USA, he's reminded of the years of basking in ovations and the acclaim of huge crowds as he sang professional opera—the so-called good life.

One thing he learned from those years: *Fame and fortune, without Jesus, can never fill the emptiness or satisfy the longing in a person's heart.*

That call Bill had "blown" was revealed to his mother before his birth. In the small church his father pastored, his mother had been deeply touched as the gifted five-year-old son of a visiting evangelist sang. She felt the Lord impressing on her that she would have a son who would be "a singer and bless many around the world."

How she needed that assurance during Bill's teen years!

Bill says that he—as children often do—decided what he wanted to do with his life. When eleven years old, he decided he'd be a juvenile delinquent! "And I had a lot of talent for the job," he says. His parents suffered through those next few years as they saw their son constantly getting into trouble. When afraid of being caught, Bill would pray, "Lord, don't let anything happen to me. I'll become a Christian when I get really old."

In the church his father pastored, the youth group consisted of one other boy and Bill. One day his father called him into his study and bargained with him. "If you'll go to that large Presbyterian church near us every Sunday morning and evening, and the youth meeting every Wednesday night, you won't have to attend my church," he told Bill. Bill gladly accepted his proposal. At that church, Bill says he learned "how to put on the 'holy-joe' outfit." Parents would say, "Oh Bill, I wish my son was as good a Christian as you." That went on for five years—"years in which I received tremendous Bible teaching," Bill says. "But I wasn't a Christian. In church I posed as a Christian; out of church, I was back into trouble."

Bill grew up knowing the consequences of his sin if he died: eternal separation from God and everything good. *Man is destined to die once, and after that to face judgment* (Hebrews 9:27). *The wages of sin is death...* (Romans 6:23). One day in the midst of his teenage rebellion, God's Spirit graphically reminded him of that. He ran to the pastor's office. There on his knees he cried and begged the Lord to take away his sin. Of that experience, Bill says, "My burden of sin was replaced with an indescribable peace. And like Dad, the same day Jesus became my Savior, I also felt God call me into His ministry."

For his final two years of high school, Bill attended a Christian school. "There I had the honor of being chosen captain of the basketball team." But when chosen to sing baritone in the school's male quartet, "I considered that an even greater honor," he says.

Following high school and starting a career job, his one great desire was still to be a gospel singer. In 1963, his company sent him to Denver for further training. There he was asked to serve as president of the career and college class of the church he attended. Bill describes the class secretary as "the beautiful Marie Ward...."

Bill and Marie were married that year and moved to Seattle. The music director of their church, Bud Tutmarc, a man heavily involved in the city's gospel music scene, mentored Bill as they worked together.

In those years Bill had a compelling drive to share Jesus Christ in song—always old-time gospel songs. Others, studying and trying desperately to get into opera, would sing high classical selections, and Bill would taunt with, "Why don't you sing real music?" Unfortunately, singing gospel music and his churchgoing habit made him feel more spiritual than other singers. "Had I taken inventory of my life," Bill confesses, "I would've realized that I was losing my first love for Jesus and becoming less dependent on Jesus and more and more dependent on Bill Harness."

One night, in discouragement, Bill prayed with Marie. His prayer: "God, show us what You want us to do with the voice You've given me." The next morning Leonard Moore, conductor of the Seattle Chorale, phoned and asked Bill to sing tenor in a chorale concert. Bill was aware that the best singers in the Seattle area sang with the chorale.

Bill was elated. During the rehearsal, Leonard said to him, "Where have you been? You have twenty times more potential than these people you're singing with." The other three soloists had master's degrees, taught voice lessons at a university level, and sang professional opera. *How can I possibly be as good as he says? I've never even seriously studied voice*, Bill thought.

Bill had always tended to ignore compliments about his voice. But here was a man he held in high esteem telling him, "You have got to do something with this voice." Bill felt God was saying, "You must do this." But he wondered, *What does "this" mean? And where will it lead me?*

After the concert, local newspapers gave Bill tremendous reviews. That encouraged him to do something. *But what?* A small article in the newspaper caught his attention. In five weeks the Metropolitan Opera would hold auditions in Seattle for tenors. The age limit for tenors—no older than thirty.

That meant now or never for him. *I'll do it!* he decided. Leonard agreed to help him. "How many arias do you know?" Leonard asked, and Bill replied, "None."

"Well," Leonard sighed, "you'll have to work super hard—but you can do it! You'll need to master at least five arias."

If mastering at least five arias wasn't enough of a challenge, Leonard also told him, "And you'll have to sing in three different languages." From the public library Bill checked out music and records of French, Italian, and English arias. Leonard helped him with pronunciation and grammar. At home Bill practiced for hours and hours….

But no one told Bill that he was also supposed to know the *meaning* of the words he sang. So at the audition, not realizing he was singing a tragedy, he threw his arms around, smiled, and acted happy. The audience loved it! *It's a sure thing,* he thought. *I've won!*

But he was not one of the three chosen. A chorus of *boos* from the audience brought the judge, the Metropolitan Chorus master himself, on stage. "Ladies and gentlemen, this is the voice I've been looking for," he began, "but this man knows nothing about what he's doing. You people must get behind him."

Discouraged, Bill prayed, *Lord, this must not be what You want for me.* Two days later the audition chairman phoned saying that the people in Seattle had raised $900 for Bill to take voice lessons.

And so it was that in 1972, he began lessons with a former Metropolitan Opera star. In the spring, after auditioning with the San Francisco Opera, he was invited to go to San Francisco for intensive training. That summer he learned the opera *La Boheme* in seventeen days and sang the tenor lead for 22,000 people at the San Francisco Stern Grove. Newspapers gave him rave reviews. And from there it was all the way up! The head of the San Francisco Opera told him, "Bill, I'll do everything in my power to get you into opera—if that's what you want."

Bill—who called himself "the self-appointed president of the I-Hate-Opera Society"—gave a resounding "Yes! That's what I want."

Things happened fast after that. He quit his career job. The opera raised $20,000 to get him started. He'd spend a month of six- to seven-hour days in training, then go on tour. Through the years, Bill sang with many famous opera singers—Leontyne Price, Joan Sutherland, Birgit Nilsson, Jerome Hines, among others. Singing with Beverly Sills resulted in international reviews.

I'll be "salt" to these needy people in the opera world, Bill told himself. But that didn't happen. He was away from family—both his wife and children *and* his Christian family, sometimes for a stretch of eleven months at a time. Instead of being a testimony to his colleagues, he adopted their lifestyle—even became a leader. His living in sin broke Marie's heart and was fast breaking up their marriage. And he was also having problems with their children. Bill found that *a person cannot know the Light of the world and live in the darkness of the world and be happy.*

In 1977, Bill sang the title role in the opera *Faust*. Jerome Hines, with whom he had made his debut in the Metropolitan

Opera, also sang in *Faust*. Jerome was a Christian. And it was to Jerome that Bill spoke the words, "I need to talk..."

Bill went home, determined to fix up his life. He knew the mechanical things to do: begin reading the Word again, start fellowshipping with Christians, mend his marriage, solve the problems with his children—and stop sinning!

He tried and fell flat on his face. His endeavors resulted in a three-week depression so deep that he didn't even want to live. In that state, he did something that he says "was beyond my power to do." He called out to God, "You take it all—my life, my voice, my career." He had no assurance that doing that would win him back the love and respect of his wife and children. But he didn't bargain with God. "I just gave everything to Him," Bill says.

That evening the Lord spoke to Bill. No writing on the wall or thunder from heaven, but he knew it was God speaking. He impressed on him to go back to his first love—singing gospel songs.

"And still I had the audacity to argue with Him," Bill confesses. *Lord, how can I do that? When singing gospel, sometimes I'd get $25, sometimes $100, sometimes a handshake and a thank-you. I have five children and a wife to support. And besides, I have no church contacts. No one knows that years ago...*

The Lord was silent. He wasn't impressed with Bill's arguments. He had spoken!

The following Monday, a man from California phoned Bill. "I read in the *San Francisco Examiner* that you used to do gospel concerts...." Apologetically, he added, "Do you think you could come to California and sing a gospel concert?"

"I must have risen six inches out of my chair!" Bill says.

That week, five people called, asking him to do gospel concerts. But more miraculously than that, the Lord showed Himself as the Healer of depression, broken hearts, and broken relationships. He put Marie and Bill's marriage back together beautifully.

Today Marie travels with Bill in this faith ministry of presenting the Lord Jesus in song. Since they have no guarantee of salary, Bill says, "It's exciting to look into the future and say, 'There's no way, absolutely no way whatsoever, we can meet our bills and eat, too.' Yet the Lord Jesus is on our side, and He has never failed us.

"As we're getting older, the wear and tear of going out weekends is sometimes a bit tough. Sometimes I think, *If we only did normal things, we'd make more money and have more time to ourselves.* But the concerts have become more than just a singing ministry. People are blessed; some are saved; some are even healed. This makes me know I can't quit. Singing for the God of the universe is far more exciting than it ever was singing for the god of this puny world."

Bill now realizes that just as Romans 8:28 says, the Lord has used all that has happened in his life to allow him to minister with music in a special way. Before going through the opera experience, people would say to him, "You have such a beautiful voice"—but now they come to him with tears in their eyes and tell him that God touched their life through his singing and sharing. "I consider that the highest compliment anyone can receive," Bill says.

"Our travels lead us throughout the United Sates and Canada. We have also had ten concerts in South Africa, six trips to former Communist countries, and many trips to prisons. Our heart is to use music as a tool to change hearts for our Lord Jesus Christ."

More about Bill Harness:

Bill's testimony of salvation begins with his parents. Despite the mid-Depression years, his father had a good job. Life was good and stable for them. Then his mother upset their stability. Someone invited her to a church that met in a small, run-down building. She went and gave her life to Jesus. She was anxious for her husband to join her in her faith, but he wanted nothing to do with a church that met "on the other side of the tracks." She prayed…and finally, two years later, he went to church with her. That day he not only met Jesus as Savior, but this man who had no church background felt God's call to the ministry.

Go to www.williamharness.com for more information on Bill Harness.

Chapter 9

The Lovings Tell Their Story

Ed and Aretta Loving

> Before Paul was a Christian, he obeyed the light he had; after he became a Christian he obeyed the Light he had!
> —*Dr. Donnie Gamble*

In Awaland, the men always eat before the women do. They also walk ahead of them on the trail—carrying bows and arrows to protect them in case enemies suddenly appear. So in keeping with their fashion of "men first," Ed goes first here…

So What Is Truth?

Ed Loving

This group claims, "We have the truth!" That group claims, "No, we have the truth!" And still another, "No, we have the truth!" And on and on…

So what is truth? I asked myself.

In my junior year at Virginia Tech, that question led me to begin reading the New Testament. I set aside twenty minutes each morning and faithfully read from God's Word.

I remember the day I came to 2 Corinthians 5:17: *Therefore if any man be in Christ, he is a new creature: old things are passed away; behold, all things are become new,* from the King James Bible.

After reading those words, I just about jumped out of my chair. *Hey, that's what's happened to me,* I said to myself. *My life has changed since I read this book!*

Later God challenged me to *go into all the world and preach the good news…* (Mark 16:15). I felt a quiet inner voice speaking to me. *My son, are you willing to take the good news to people overseas who have never heard it?*

"Sure, Lord," I answered flippantly. But the Lord wouldn't let me read further until I faced up to His question.

I got down on my knees and told Him that yes, by His grace, I would serve Him overseas. After that, peace permeated my whole being. And I'm grateful that God sent Aretta into my life to go with me!

Where There Are No Oxen

Aretta Loving

And I'm grateful that God sent Ed into my life to go with me! Despite that, I remember a time when I was grumbling about him. *Why can't he be less frugal?*

Ed is a conservative spender; so am I. But his frugality bordered on stinginess; mine, I told myself, was just *being a good steward of God's gifts. Why can't he relax a bit more*? Ed has a strong work ethic; so do I. But his preoccupation with work I labeled workaholism; mine, *redeeming the time.*

The week passed with me becoming more and more discontent. Then I picked up a magazine... "Feeling unappreciative of your husband?" the article read. "Make a list of ten things you are thankful for about him. Every morning and every night for ten days, thank God for each of those ten things. By the end of the ten days, you will see your husband in a new light. You might even recognize some of those qualities that attracted you to him when you decided to marry him," the author concluded.

"Well, it's worth a try," I grudgingly admitted.

But as I tried to make my list, I couldn't think of anything to write down. I was alarmed at what grumbling had done to me! Grumbling had closed my mind to anything I was thankful for about my husband. It had dried up feelings of thankfulness for him.

"Lord, help me!" I prayed. "You command us to be thankful. That's not a suggestion, not an option. Help me, Lord, to be thankful for my husband."

Suddenly two things came to mind. *Hmmm, was it the Lord's sense of humor that caused me to think of these?*

1. He's not a spendthrift!
2. He's not lazy!

I scratched my memory to find things for my list! I added two more things:

3. He provides well for his family.
4. He loves God.

That will have to do for today, I decided. I thanked God sincerely that night and the next morning for those four things. In the evening I watched him playing with our two small daughters. He laughed. I added numbers five and six.

5. His hearty laugh—I've always loved it!
6. He loves our daughters.

And that reminded me...

7. He loves me.

By the end of the week, my list had grown to not just ten points, but over twenty! Along with that growth, a renewed appreciation and love for my husband had budded along with the promise of once again unfolding in full bloom.

Two things on that list of twenty were: his sense of humor and the fact that he is faithful! Yes, he has been faithful to the Lord and to me! Even the thought of his being unfaithful to me has never existed in our over fifty years of marriage! And we enjoy laughing together, knowing that *a cheerful heart is good medicine* (Proverbs 17:22). And yes, God commands us to *rejoice always, pray constantly, give thanks in all circumstances: for this is the will of God in Christ Jesus for you* (1 Thessalonians 5:16–18, RSV).

I reckon that when God gave that command, He knew women like me would be tempted to grumble about our husbands. He also knew what giving thanks for them would do for me—and for you.

***More about Ed and Aretta Loving*:**

Ed and I are members of Wycliffe Bible translators. We served in Papua New Guinea, where we worked with the Awa people to translate the New Testament and a book of Old Testament Bible stories into their language. We have been married over fifty years. We have two daughters: Karen Loving Branagan and Treesa Loving Hause. (See the following two chapters.)

For the last decade-plus we have lived at the JAARS Center, Wycliffe's support center in Waxhaw, North Carolina. Ed does editing, as I also do, for various Wycliffe colleagues here and elsewhere on request. He has also done Scripture checking by e-mail for a Nigerian team of men who are translating the Bible into their mother tongue. In 2011 we spent six weeks in Nigeria working as translation consultants with Nigerian translators from the Nigerian Bible Translation Trust. Currently Ed works in Vernacular Media Services, editing short Bible scripts that will be translated by people whose mother tongue is not English.

I have published:

- *Slices of Life: Stories and Devotions from a Bible Translator,*

2000, YWAM Publishing (translated into Russian, Chinese, and Polish).

• *Zoeter dan Honing*, 2002, Wycliffe Bijbelvertalers Nederlan.

• *Together We Can! A Mosaic of Stories and Devotions Displaying the Impact of God's Word*, 2007, Vol. 1, 2006, Harvest Day Books.

I continue to enjoy my husband's sense of humor! One recent example: He was making himself a cheese sandwich. He looked at the cheese and said, "I'm not the last one to cut on this cheese." When I asked him how he knew that, he replied, "Because this cheese is cut crooked."

I knew how it bothers him when his bread is not cut straight, or a tomato is sliced crooked. So, long ago I resigned from bread cutting and tomato slicing for him.

"So? Will that cause you to become ill?" I replied, and we both laughed.

I have cut his hair ever since we were engaged. Not a job I can say I enjoy, but he was never pleased with any barber he went to. "

"As of today, I resign from cutting your cheese—and the next time I cut your hair, I'm going to cut it crooked!" I told him. But I've not done that yet….

Chapter 10

What Brings Joy and Brightness into a Life?

Karen Loving Branagan

> The etymology of illustrious makes it clear that a shining glow (both literal and figurative) has long been associated with the word. Illustrious ultimately derives from the Latin verb *lustrare*, meaning "to purify, make bright."
>
> —Merriam-Webster's *365 New Words Calendar*

Karen, a three-year-old girl with a glowing face, announced, "I got new shoes!"

On a Sunday morning walking to church down a dusty dirt road in Papua New Guinea, we met a coworker also on her way to church. And it was to her that Karen made her announcement. Then she proceeded to announce that she had a new dress, and then she lifted her skirt and announced, "I got new panties!"

Well, at her age, I guess one can get by with that. Of course, she doesn't remember that, but she's often reminded of it, as her mom—that's me—tells her, "Today I got new shoes!" or "Today I got a new blouse!" And then we laugh together over that incident that occurred long ago on that dusty road to church.

Today what makes Karen's face glow is not new shoes. It's Jesus in her! Karen received Jesus as her Savior at five years of age when attending a daily Vacation Bible School in Papua New Guinea. She graduated from high school in PNG, then went to the University of Virginia and graduated with a nursing degree. She met a handsome young man named Lyle Branagan there as he was studying for his doctorate in engineering.

"Her smile was what attracted me," Lyle says. They were married in 1960 and now have three sons—one in the army; one attending postgraduate school at UVA, following in his dad's footsteps; and one in high school. She and Lyle are both active in their church. After they married, Lyle worked in New York. When an opportunity for a job in North Carolina came up, Lyle applied. He was competing for the job with a couple other PhDs. But he says, "I knew I'd be the one they hired for the job because my mother-in-law was praying me into it." They live just an hour away from us in North Carolina.

Karen once told me that she wished we lived closer so I could come over even more often and tell her how to arrange things in her kitchen. "Karen, you know you wouldn't like that," I told her.

Her reply was, "Oh, Mom, I know I wouldn't. But I'd sure enough like the opportunity to not like it!"

Karen has always been a busy housewife, besides working part-time in a nearby hospital. One Christmas season, the whole family went to Costa Rica—a trip financed by Karen's hospital paychecks.

Karen and Lyle make opportunities to spend weekends and vacation time with their family. All three of their sons earned the Boy Scout of Honor award before the age of fifteen. During those years, both parents were heavily involved with their sons in Boy Scouts.

Karen has participated in Bible Study Fellowship for many years, and the many friends she has made through the study also brings light into her life. But above and beyond that, the knowledge she's gained of the Word through the study has also brought and continues to bring more of the Light into her life!

More about Karen Branagan:
See under More about . . . in Chapter 9.

Chapter 11

Double Exposure

Treesa Loving Hause

Treesa Hause is the girl that bees and chickens obey. When three years old, she was playing in the yard and a bee stung her. The same day, a mother hen, feeling threatened by her coming too close to her brood of "peeps and fluffs," pecked her. For the rest of the day and for the next few days, she walked around looking every bee and every chicken in our yard directly in the eye and saying to them, "Don't do dat!"[1]

And they obeyed her. She was never stung by a bee or pecked by a hen again!

"I remember the hymn Mom used to sing to me when I was a little girl:

When we walk with the Lord in the light of His Word,
What a glory He sheds on our way!
While we do His good will,
He abides with us still,
And to all who will trust and obey.
Trust and obey, for there's no other way
To be happy in Jesus but to trust and obey.[2]

"And I've endeavored by His grace to *walk with the Lord in the light of His Word* as that song says."

Now Treesa is a grown woman with a faithful, loving husband, Mike, two beautiful daughters, and a handsome son. They served for twenty-five years in Manila, Philippines, at a school called Faith Academy.[3] All three of their children were born in Manila and loved growing up in the Philippines. Their two daughters, Alyssa and Kendra, both graduated from Faith Academy. Alyssa graduated from Lee University in Tennessee. Kendra is in her second year there.

Singing with the children at their church in Manila for Saturday Kid's Club was one of Treesa's favorite things to do. "Joy is holding hands in a long chain and dancing with over four hundred children as they sing," Treesa says. "It's a great thing to praise the Lord, walking in the light of God. *Walk, walk, walk, walk in the light, walking in the light of God.*" Then she asks, "What does it mean to walk in the light? I learned a bit of what it means when we were asked to leave Faith Academy Manila and accept an assignment at Faith Academy Davao."

Is God calling us to leave Manila and work at Faith Academy in Davao? Mike and Treesa wondered. They really liked serving at Faith Academy and raising their children in Manila. And they also liked the house and neighborhood where they lived. They had made a lot of friends and had been instrumental in seeing their neighbor come to the Lord Jesus before he died.

"And," Treesa says, "we loved our ministry to the people who lived in the slums down in the valley below us, as well as our church, New Hope to Asia. In fact, we loved living right where we were."

But God began nudging them to move out of their comfort zone, and they began praying for Him to open the door if indeed He was calling them to a different place. About that time, a visiting pastor prayed over them at church and, knowing nothing about their situation, said he felt God was leading them into a new ministry.

Not long after that, they were asked if they would be willing to move to Davao for Mike to be the principal at the K–12th grade missionary school there. An open door? Yes! "That assured us that indeed God was asking us to leave Manila and go to Davao," Treesa says. Was it easy? No. But what a chance to trust and walk in obedience in the light God put before them.

Before Mike flew to Davao to look for a house, a friend encouraged Treesa by telling her, as he prayed for their house, he felt the Lord saying He had a house for them "with space and light and an openness of spirit—a place that would be a blessing and an encouragement to others." Proverbs 13:9 says, *The light of the righteous shines brightly*. Mike and Treesa's prayer from Philippians 2 has always been that their lives would reflect the Lord's love—that they would shine out like beacon lights holding out the Word of life in a dark world. And we've also prayed that our home would be full of light—spiritually and physically too.

"After Mike found a house and signed a contract," Treesa says, "we packed up the car and Mike drove three days and took two ferries to get to Davao."

The morning Mike was scheduled to arrive in Davao, in his devotions he read from Psalm 112:7–8 in *The Living Bible*: "*He does not fear bad news, nor live in dread of what may happen. For he is settled in his mind that Jehovah will take care of him. That is why he is not afraid, but can calmly face his foes.*"

That afternoon Treesa's friend Ruth reminded her that the house they were supposed to move into when they first arrived in Manila to serve at Faith did not work out for them either. But then God provided their family with a wonderful house right near the school.

"As Ruth and I were talking, Mike phoned me to say the landlady had just backed out of the lease he had signed. He was about to arrive in Davao and move in to the house—but God had a different plan.

"I went back to Psalm 112:4–6," Treesa says, "and I was amazed at God's specific word to us: *Even in darkness light dawns for the upright...* (one version of the Bible says, "*light will come bursting in*")*...for the gracious and compassionate and righteous....*" As I read the words "*light will come bursting in*," I saw it as another chance to trust and obey even when things did not look good, and wait for the light before we took the next step."

God continued to give Treesa peace and joy, and He also gave her a dream before she flew to Davao. In the dream she walked into a beautiful house. "As I stepped into the bedroom I gazed in awe at the beauty of the light shining through the windows and the ocean shimmering in blue and green. The waves lapped gently against the glass windows, and lying down on the bed I fell into a deep sleep. When I woke up, the Lord gave me the words, *I am surrounding you with an ocean of peace.* And I knew the peace and joy I had was definitely from Him. *What a glory He sheds on our way.* Yes the glory of the Lord was in that place," Treesa says. "I knew God was taking care of us.

"Isaiah 12:2 in the *New International Version* says, *Surely God is my salvation; I will trust and not be afraid.* As Mike sought the Lord and prayed over the Davao campus, God gave him a picture of big vessels taking off like huge jets, and he saw an explosion of light. He felt as though God was saying that something big is going out to war in the heavenlies. *God is going to fight for you and give freedom in the Spirit. God is going to move on the campus in Davao.*

"Because of that promise and the dream the Lord gave me, I wish I could say I did not worry at all about a house," Treesa said. "But I still had moments when I felt as though I was walking in darkness. At those times, I cried out to the Lord for *His* light. Another beautiful verse the Lord gave me was from Hosea 2:14, where God says He that He will allure us, speak tenderly to us, and make the Valley of Achor a door of Hope.

"Before we left, our church in Manila had gathered around us and sent us out to Davao with their blessing—and our tears. Yes, we have new hope in Davao because we have the God of hope living within us. We have walked through times when the light seemed dim but God's light was always before us. Isaiah 12:5 says, *Sing to the LORD for he has done glorious things....* One of those 'glorious things' that He did for us was to give us a house filled with light."

Yes, indeed! God gave both Mike and Treesa light to their move—a double exposure of light! Their prayer from Philippians 2 had always been that they would shine out like beacon lights, holding out the Word of life in a dark world. And they always prayed that their home would be full of light spiritually —and physically, too—and be a blessing to others.

More about Treesa Hause:

See under More about . . . in Chapter 10.

1 See *Slices of Life*, Chapter 5, for a fuller account of this story.

2 "When We Walk with the Lord" is now in the public domain. The lyrics were composed by Daniel Tower, 1850–1919; the words by John H. Sammis, 1846–1919.

3 Faith Academy is a school for MKs Their students come from the Philippines as well as other countries in that part of the world. Those from other countries live in a dorm with house parents.

Chapter 12

"Washa Doin' Taday, Tee-imm?"

Tim Roberts

O Christ, Lamb of God, slain for the sin of the whole world, with penitent heart I come to Your cross, pleading for mercy and forgiveness. My sins—and they are many—have added to the burden of Your suffering and have nailed You to the accursed tree. For me You tasted the agony of the utter darkness that I might not perish, but have everlasting life. —*The Lutheran Book of Prayer*

It was Sunday morning at Virginia Tech during Tim's sophomore year. He was bored. *Isn't there something more interesting to do than sit here and study?* he asked himself. *I studied all day Saturday and I'm tired of studying. Besides, I'm pretty much caught up on my studies.*

As he was thinking that, he looked up from his desk, and there stood one of his classmates at his open door—very drunk!

"Washa doin' taday, Tee-imm?"

"Nothing in particular, Charlie. I was just sitting here thinking about what I was going to do. More studying maybe, and then—well, I guess I'll go to bed early for a change."

"Come along wish me, Tee-im," Charlie slurred. "Ah'sh gwoin' ta Schunday school."

"You're going *where*, Charlie? Did you say you're going to *Sunday school*?"

"Yesh, Ah'sh gwoin' to Schunday school, Tee-im. Thash what Ah shaid. Ah'sh gwoin' to Schunday school."

A drunk going to Sunday school?! Hmmm. Now that might be interesting to observe, Tim decided. He'd never been to Sunday school; he had never read the Bible. He was reared in a happy home of very respectable, wonderful, and honored parents, but his family weren't churchgoers. Sunday was always just another day in their home.

"I knew Charlie would be feeling badly by then for having gotten drunk. Good he's going to Sunday school. So why not go along with him and check it out?" Tim decided.

The teacher was a former athlete, and most of the attendees were members of InterVarsity Christian Fellowship.

Christian? What's that? Tim wondered.

"I listened attentively as the teacher read chapter after chapter on a particular topic. And I found it interesting. Interesting enough that I continued to go. After three months Charlie dropped out."

But Tim—for a reason he couldn't understand—continued to go, week after week.

"That was the first time I had sat under Bible reading and teaching, and I continued for almost a year. Those students recognized that I was totally ignorant of the Scriptures. They strongly urged me to attend InterVarsity Christian Fellowship at Campus in the Woods in Canada. I went, and there I heard the Bible expounded by Bible college and seminary professors for two weeks. It became obvious I was not getting it. A cabin mate recognized my plight and said he was like that once. 'Then I realized that if Jesus Christ took my sin upon Himself, dying in my place, then I killed Him.'

"It was that statement—I killed Him—that opened my understanding of who Jesus Christ was, why He came, and what He accomplished on the cross. And that morning, sitting on a rock overlooking the lake with sunlight reflecting off of it, I confessed I was a sinner and asked Jesus—the Son-Light—to be my Savior."

More about Tim Roberts:

Tim was born in Norfolk, Virginia. In high school he was active in sports but "not much of a student," he says, "which became evident when I graduated mid-year." He first attended a community college before going to Virginia Tech in the fall. His second year there he ran track. He confesses, "That, of course, resulted in my flunking out!"

Eventually Tim graduated from there as a second lieutenant. He was drafted into the service and applied to go overseas but was turned down. His assignment was running a firing range on the Atlantic Coast near Ocean City, Maryland.

Tim says, "The pastor of the Presbyterian church there in Maryland was right on target with the gospel. So, Sunday found me in his church."

There he met his future wife, Fran Cropper. He proposed and Fran said yes, but Tim later broke the engagement. His reason: how can a graduate with an agriculture degree who never farmed nor had a farm support a family? Shortly after that, Tim was accepted into medical school at the University of Virginia.

After two years there, he returned to Ocean City and again asked Fran if she would marry him. Tim shows his sense of humor by saying, "No good reason for her to say yes, but she did!

"With foreign missions burning in our hearts, when a former IVCF attendee of Campus in the Woods in Canada told me of a need for a doctor in Afghanistan, we filled it. I had taken a four-year surgical residency, which was fully used in our four years there. After we returned I continued surgery in the USA."

Tim and Fran have been married over fifty years and have four children and nineteen grandchildren, all of whom are following the Lord.

Tim, now retired, enjoys spending time with his family and working in his apple orchard.

Chapter 13

Out of Witchcraft Into the Light

Louise Derr

> I heard the voice of Jesus say, "I am this dark world's Light; look unto Me—thy morn shall rise, and all thy days be bright." I looked to Jesus, and I found in Him my Star, my Sun, and that Light of life I'll walk till trav'ling days are done. —*Horatius Bonar*

"Your mom has died," her dad solemnly reported to Louise.

"What a shock to me and my two younger sisters," Louise says. "We knew she had lung cancer, but death is hard for a ten-year-old to understand. It meant moving away from my dear maternal grandmother to live with an aunt and uncle and their two children in Chapel Hill, North Carolina. My dad and two sisters went to live with our paternal grandfather two houses down the street.

"What a challenge for this fifth-grader—new school, new home, loss of mother, separated from my immediate family, and recovering from serious rheumatic-fever illness. Some nights I cried myself to sleep."

A year and a half later, Louise's father married a woman with a boy and a girl. Louise was the oldest of five siblings, and they lived in the house between the relatives. "After my half brother was born," Louise says, "we moved out to a small farm. This meant changing schools my freshman year in high school. Though I was still not as strong physically as I should have been, I loved spending time outdoors."

Louise's father, wanting to know if there was life after death and if the deceased could be contacted, spoke with several pastors. None gave him encouraging answers. As a traveling salesman, he usually listened to the radio. On one trip he heard a pastor talk about contacting the dead. Through the radio station he located this pastor, a spiritualist.

"We began to hold séances in our home with visiting spiritualist mediums," Louise says. "We children, now six of us, grew up with spiritualism as a normal part of life. We stopped going to the little country Methodist church down the road as we had 'church' in our home. Dad's father, a retired United Christian missionary, tried to convince Dad he was wrong in this new belief, but he refused to listen."

Living at home during college years, Louise continued attending séances every Sunday night. "I left home right after finishing college when I married a wonderful guy. But six years later, I moved back to Chapel Hill when my marriage dissolved. Unfortunately, my rheumatic fever returned as a result of the stress. I went back to attending séances—only this time I took my little son David along with me.

"Soon I became the spiritualist medium, leading the séances. The group had grown to a dozen or more, and the spirits were actively answering questions and giving guidance. All this was amazing to this medium as the spirits controlled my thoughts and used my voice while I was in a trance."

Then a friend who formally attended the séances gave Louise a book: *The Challenging Counterfeit*, by Raphael Gasson. The book exposed spiritualism as contact with demons, rather than the departed loved ones' spirits or spirit guides. As Louise read

Gasson's book, she became aware that in Deuteronomy 18:10–12, spiritualism is labeled an *abomination.* "I wanted to get out if this was a demonic cult," Louise says, "but my parents and siblings did not want to. My boyfriend, now my husband, Harry Derr, had recently rededicated his life to Jesus. He invited me to his new church.

"On October 23, 1974, at a home Bible study at that church, I had a very real vision of black horsemen with a huge black blanket coming to smother me. With heart problems I've had because of rheumatic fever, dying would not have been a surprise. I cried out, 'Help me!' Some men in the Bible study came over, as they expected the demons would attack, and laid hands on me and prayed. Immediately the death-demons left.

"Then Jesus stood in their place! He gently spoke three words: '*Come unto Me.*' I had thought that if I ever experienced Jesus, I didn't want to be tricked again. I wanted to see the Holy Spirit in dove form on His shoulder. And there was the dove sitting on His right shoulder!

"I fell into His open arms, totally surrendering to Him. He embraced me and held me for about ten minutes. Though I didn't remember it, the people in the Bible study group said I didn't move but kept saying, '*Thank You, Jesus. Praise You, Lord!*' over and over. When I returned home that night, I boxed up all the occult books and paraphernalia I could find.

"The next morning at the school where I taught, I stopped by the principal's office. Paul was a Christian and had been praying for me for years. 'Paul,' I called."

Paul looked up, and before Louise could say anything, Paul exclaimed, "You did it!"

"Paul could see that I was glowing from my contact with Jesus!" Louise says. "After school I met with some of the same men from the Bible study the night before and gave them my box of occult books to be burned. Then I was baptized in a farm pond.

When I came up out of the water, I felt as light as a feather!

"I left the séance group, which caused a lot of disturbance in my family since I was the group's medium. My parents and siblings wanted little to do with me or my son or my new husband. For twenty years as I grew in the Lord they continued in the occult. Then Dad became ill with terminal cancer.

"Taking a leave of absence from teaching, I took the day shift in caring for Dad, as he wanted to die at home. Living only twelve miles away, it was easy to travel to my 'mission field.' I asked the Lord how to reach this rebellious MK. He had grown up in Puerto Rico, so Spanish was really his heart language. The Lord impressed upon me that Dad needed to hear the gospel in Spanish, out loud, as he would have heard it from his pastor father. I ordered the *Jesus* video in Spanish, and we watched it together.

"And the Lord led me to a Gideon Bible with Spanish and English on each page. I asked Dad to read aloud to me the book of John from that Bible. When he read John 11, he realized he was like Lazarus: bound in death from his sins and needing Jesus to set him free. He started talking to Someone in front of him, confessing he needed Jesus. Then he took a nap. A month and a half later he died as a Christian believer.

"My siblings accepted me back because I had helped care for Dad. Some of my family members are now believers; some still are involved in some aspect of the occult. My prayer for them is that they realize that Jesus died on the cross for their sins. It is a matter of life and death—having life for eternity in the beauty and peace of heaven or forever dying in the torment of hell. I pray and remind myself that we serve a God who is able to set them free! After all, He delivered both me and my husband from witchcraft, and He can do the same for my family members!

"When we let the Lord take over, He guides us into activities we never dreamed of. He will never leave us or forsake us. And we will spend eternity with Him in heaven!"

More about Louise Derr:

Today Louise and her husband, Harry, live in Waxhaw, North Carolina, near JAARS, Wycliffe Bible Translator's support center. Both she and her husband volunteer in Vernacular Media Services, a JAARS department. Louise learned the skill of audio recording on computer and is sharing the vision in spreading the Gospel orally. People from all over the world come to JAARS to be trained in Vernacular Media.

Louise received her bachelor's and master's degrees in education from UNC-Chapel Hill. For twenty-six years she taught in the North Carolina public schools. Traveling in eighteen countries around the world has given her a desire to see people everywhere discover the science in the Scriptures.

"When I retired from teaching, the Lord gave me an assignment to write about science in the Bible," Louise says. Her first book published is for elementary-aged children, *Experiencing Bible Science: An Activity Book for Children.* The second book is for any age, *Experiencing Bible Science: A Lab Book for the Young at Heart.*

The third book is in the planning stage but will be on the same topic, aimed at preschool children. Her third book contains solid scientific data along with engaging activities. It also ties in with biblical culture and history, including lots of biblical references that will pique youths' curiosity and foster their eagerness to search the Scriptures. They will find connections between the sometimes mystifying world of the Bible and their own world. The book provides plenty of room for creativity and exploration, whether students are observing insects, making a movie, or using their bodies as units of measurement. Although this book states that it is intended for middle-schoolers or older people with young hearts, much of it will be easily adaptable for younger kids as well, with some guidance. Louise has presented her science curriculum for gifted children at numerous state and national teachers' conferences.

"It has been thrilling to work directly with the Holy Spirit on these books, getting up at five o'clock in the morning. He is always there with us through the whole day if we tune in to Him."

Go to her website, www.kidsbiblescience.com, to read reviews on her books and for ordering. You may also search on the web "Experiencing Bible Science" for more sources.

Louise says of herself, "This motorcyclist, private airplane pilot, and scuba diver enjoys gardening and nature study. I was also active in Boy Scouts and the Civil Air Patrol."

Chapter 14

Investment Through Involvement

Craig Miller

> Fame and fortune, without Jesus, can never fill the emptiness or satisfy the longing in a person's heart.
>
> —*Bill Harness*

Malcolm Muggeridge was asked, "What do you want to do with the rest of your life?" and he answered, "I should like my light to shine, like a match struck in a dark, cavernous night and then flickering out."

The story below tells what one successful businessman decided he wanted to do with the rest of his life. Craig Miller begins his story[1] with: "We all have different seasons of life, and this is a very exciting season for me."

When Waxhaw, North Carolina, builder and land developer Craig Miller talks about his involvement in supporting Bible translation, his enthusiasm is contagious. Craig could be focused solely on expanding his business and making more money to support missions, but for him, *personal* involvement is just as important.

Craig has recently become involved in the JAARS Business as Mission (BAM) initiative as a board member for Word Access, the for-profit subsidiary created to help expand "Kingdom businesses" overseas through start-up capital and business planning.

Over the last year through several timely events, God has shown exactly how and where He wants Craig to become more personally involved in ministry. Reading *Halftime: Changing Your Game Plan from Success to Significance* by Bob Buford kick-started his journey. The book talks about not abandoning a God-given skill set, but instead finding ways to leverage it into kingdom work, using what God has built into your life during the previous twenty or thirty years. "It catapulted me into thinking outside my comfort zone," says Craig.

This led him to talk with Dennis Steenwyk, Business as Mission coordinator, about possible ways to use his skills. Soon after, in February 2009, a *Rev. 7* issue featuring Business as Mission (BAM) showed up in the mail. Craig says it's the first issue he's ever excitedly read from cover to cover.

"Not long after that," he continues, "David Reeves, who at that time was the JAARS president, was looking for someone with a business perspective to serve on the Word Access board, and he asked me to consider joining." The appointment has proven to be a perfect fit for both the builder and BAM.

On a recent trip to Kenya, Craig spent time with Martin Mboha of Great World Ventures Limited, a business-as-mission information technology company that received the first loan from Word Access last year. "It was exhilarating to see how committed Kenyans are to the task and truly passionate about bringing the Word of God to other people.

"It was brought to my attention afresh how someone's heart language speaks to them like no other. That really impressed upon me the tremendous value of what I might be able to contribute, and that the little things I am able to do through supporting Bible translation would certainly have good return."

Dennis Steenwyk remarks, "I would definitely say the more

involved Craig gets, the more enthused he gets. He is helping us develop training, coaching, and support for small businesses. These endeavors will link the church in *developed* countries with the church in *developing* countries in a way that will bring human dignity, alleviate poverty, and, in all, glorify God. That really is his heart."

Craig agrees, "The whole idea of helping to relieve poverty in a sustainable way is very invigorating to me personally." Linking up with JAARS to accomplish such goals brings him significant bonuses: furthering Bible translation and serving the Church.

Craig challenges businessmen to leverage their unique knowledge and experience into other people's lives. "I wouldn't be able to preach or translate the Bible or do a number of things you would traditionally think of as being beneficial to the kingdom. But helping Christians succeed in business so that they can better themselves and their community is significant.... It is very important for the Church to be relevant in society. I think that business, jobs, and employment are wonderful ways to accomplish that."

Ecclesiastes 3:1 says, *There is a time for everything, and a season for every activity under heaven.* For Craig Miller, it's his time and season to invest his God-given skills in the kingdom through Bible translation support.[2]

More about Craig Miller:

Craig is married to Sharon, and they have three children: Stephen, Crystal, and April. They live near Charlotte, North Carolina.

As director and president of Kinterra Strategies, and owner of the Kinterra Group, a family of companies working in partnership with Kinterra Strategies, Craig helps improve the lives of underprivileged people and conveys the gospel to people through his business development. He has over twenty-five years of experience in custom home building, land development, and property management. He is a businessman who is active in his local church and in several other Christian and community organizations. He is dedicated to serving Jesus through business and in all areas of ministry. His business experience, his community leadership, and his vision and passion to help lift people out of poverty are real assets he brings to the leadership of Kinterra Strategies.

1 Craig Miller's story appeared in the Spring 2010 issue (Volume 5, Issue 2) of *Rev. 7*, a publication of JAARS, Wycliffe's Support Center. Carol Brinneman edits *Rev. 7*, as well as editing books for other writers and teaching writing classes. *All the World Is Singing: Glorifying God through the Worship Music of the Nations*, by Frank Fortunato with Paul Neeley and Carol Brinneman, is scheduled to be translated into Chinese.

2 The above article was written by Heather Eastwood, who serves as public relations coordinator for the JAARS Business as Mission (BAM) team.

Chapter 15

"Pray for My Wife!"

Umahto

> Some people change when they see the light, others when they feel the heat. —*Caroline Schoeder*

"Honey Old Man,[1] my wife's been sick for two moons. And I want you to ask God to heal her!"

To "Honey Old Man"—what the Awas called Ed because they couldn't pronounce his name and one day that heard Aretta call him "Honey"—Umahto's request sounded more like a command than a request. It was our second field term in Papua New Guinea, and we were once again living in an Awa village and working with the Awa people to translate the New Testament. One day Umahto, an important leader in the village, came to Ed's study with his wife.

By that time the Lord had enabled us to start an indigenous[2] church there in the village. So Ed told Umahto to take his request to the village church elders since that was now their responsibility rather than Ed's. He went away disgruntled, but since he had no other choice, he went to see the elders of the church.

And they quickly told him, "Right now you're still seeing the local shaman[3] about your wife's health, aren't you? You must finish or stop what you're doing with him first, then you come back and we'll talk with you both and pray for her."

After another week Umahto brought his wife back to the elders and said they had stopped going to the shaman. The elders talked with the couple and encouraged them to call on Jesus Christ as Savior and Lord. Umahto and his wife prayed to receive Christ. Then the elders prayed for the wife to be healed.

Normally after they've been sick, Awa women go through a body strengthening process that includes gradually taking longer walks and carrying heavier loads each day until they get their strength back. Umahto's wife hadn't left the village for almost two months, but early the next day, she took her large *billum*—hand-woven bark-string bag—and walked 1,000 feet down the mountain to her garden.

There she spent a couple of hours digging up sweet potatoes and putting them into her string bag. Then she picked up that heavy load—weighing from fifty to seventy pounds—put the bag strap against her forehead, and trudged back up the mountain trail to the village. When the village people saw or later heard about what Umahto's wife had done that day, they all knew that God had miraculously healed her.

More about Umahto:

Umahto is now with the Lord! You may read another story about him in *Together We Can!* at the back of the book under "About the Author" section—"Real People Eat Sweet Potato"—a story that shows Umahto's sense of humor.

1 Later, they added "Old Man"—which was an honor since they respect older people.

2 An indigenous church is a church that is self-governing, self-expressing, self-supporting, and self-propagating.

3 A "witch doctor"—also called a "shaman"—was originally referred to a

type of healer who treated ailments believed to be caused by witchcraft. "A shaman is a person who interacts with both the normal world and the world of spirits, acting a sort of intermediary between the two. Shamans are common in many tribal cultures, although shamanism may also exist in other types of culture. The shaman is often responsible for both the physical and spiritual health of people, and may also be called upon to invoke spirits for aid, or to predict the future and interpret omens" (from Wikipedia and other sources).

Chapter 16

From Serving the Devil to Serving God in Bible Translation

Naphtaly Mattah

It is as though an angel stands behind us throwing light over our shoulder onto Jesus who faces us. —*Anonymous*

He was born into poverty. When just a small child, he decided to invest all his energy in education. "I was sure education was the tool for combating poverty," he says. "In my country, Kenya, being a 'big man' is a goal we all strive to reach. Surely, I told myself, *I will become a big man, a successful man, once I complete my education.*"

So Naphtaly Mattah climbed the ladder of education—primary school, secondary school, high school—assured that once he reached the top, he would arrive into the "liberating plenty of the world." And Naphtaly did arrive in that land of plenty! By the time he reached university, he had found there were plenty of bad things that, he says, "controlled my life." He was into drinking and taking drugs. He was leading an immoral lifestyle. He had become a strike leader in riots at his university. "Sometimes I had doubts about my activities. *But, surely,* I thought, *my education, which had now become my god, would deliver me.*"

One evening, reeking of alcohol and still feeling in his body the effects from his heavy drinking of the night before, he went into a hotel restaurant to pick up food he had ordered. There an elderly Kikuyu-speaking woman approached him. "With love beaming from her eyes, she confronted me with the words, 'Young man, did you know Jesus loves you and that He died to save you?'

"Mum, look at me," Naphtaly replied. "Look at the mess I am. I'm sure you can see that it's too late for someone like me to be saved."

Ignoring his stench, she continued, "My son, don't despise yourself. This Jesus I'm telling you about knows everything about you. Despite how you are, despite what you've done, He loves you. There is nothing *you* can do to change your life. But the all-powerful God is able to change you. And I'm here to tell you how He can do that."

Rather than answer her, Naphtaly took his packet of Embassy King Cigarettes out of his pocket and laid them on the table. She grabbed them, and holding them behind her, she continued talking to him about Jesus and how He alone could change his messed-up life.

As excuse after excuse rolled off Naphtaly's lips, the lady with love in her eyes smothered them with her words of love from a God of love. And that night that little old woman led him to a life-changing encounter with Jesus Christ.

For many years Naphtaly wondered if the Kikuyu woman was an angel. She wore no halo of light, but she led Naphtaly to the source of Light. Many, many years later she phoned Naphtaly. She had been praying for him ever since that evening.

Naphtaly testifies that "the message that little old lady gave me changed my life. I did not go to counseling, but that very night, drugs, alcohol, and smoking, as well as other sinful habits, left my life forever." After Naphtaly's conversion, God led him to a lovely Christian woman. He and Nereah were married in 1993.

"I sat under many pastors' teachings and learned about prayer and fasting—and so much more. I read many books. And I read the Bible over and over, and I'm still doing that."

After Naphtaly's conversion, a burning desire came into his heart to tell his friends about the saving grace of Jesus—the One who had so drastically changed his life. "I was an evangelist," he says. He went out to Mfangano Island in Lake Victoria to reach his people.

"My people were animists. When they constructed a boat, they cut a tree and let it fall on someone. Then the boat spirits would tell them how to wage war. Poverty and hopelessness described my people, and I began to tell what God had done for me."

And the results of his telling—people would cry out to demons to leave them, then they'd fall to the ground. The sick were healed as they came to "prayer closets" for Naphtaly to pray for them.

Naphtaly rejoices that "during that time my dad and mother, my brother, and many friends came to know the Lord Jesus."

God gave Naphtaly a burden to evangelize his own Suba[1] people there on Mfangano Island. He organized teams and took them to the island to preach—and God honored His Word powerfully. But to his disappointment, those who made decisions fell back. That made him realize that unless the Word of God addressed the Suba people in their own culture, in their heart language, evangelism was not going to be functional in their society.

"When asked to do translation, I felt this was an interruption. But I agreed to do it for one year. I began by using an old typewriter. After a year, I extended my commitment to two years. Nineteen years later, with the help of Boniface that whole time, and help from Jeremiah part of that time, on April 15, 2011, we dedicated the New Testament! People bought 800 copies before they even arrived, and on the day of dedication 1,600 were bought.

"I was honored when the pastors in our community and Bible Translation and Literacy (BTL) in Nairobi asked me to be the project leader. That was in 1992. Our language had never been documented, so the first thing was linguistic research and writing papers. Many people helped me—especially Ed Loving, Language Programs Coordinator, serving under BTL.

"Many pastors were longing for Scripture, but none could imagine that the Bible could be written by human beings. They seemed to think it was a book that dropped somewhere from heaven, and it was written in our neighbor's language.

"So my first job was to prove that the Bible could be written—in our language—so, using an old typewriter, I chose the book of Jonah to translate first, since we are islanders and therefore fishermen. This caused the people to realize that, *Yes, God is speaking directly to us, not through interpreters, but in our own language.* God ceased to be a foreign God; He became *our* God.

"Doing the translation wasn't always smooth-going. We saw the devil build up hurdles against the translating of God's Word. But the white horse of Revelation 19:11–16 whose name is 'the Word of God' was able to jump those hurdles! One of those hurdles was pain on the left side of my body that could have killed me. After the dedication the pain stopped.

"Wherever Jesus is exalted, He does not leave things the same; He is a life-changer," Naphtaly says. "I want more of Him in my life—I want to be a vessel wholly dedicated to spreading the Gospel. My food is to do the will of Him who sent me."

More about Naphtaly:

Naphtaly received an MA in translation studies from NEGST in Nairobi. Nereah received her MA in Christian education from there at the same time. Their children are Calvary, Joy, Zion, Sinai, and baby Harmony Msiza, born in 2011. Calvary and Joy were selected to attend national high schools (an extreme honor in Kenya), and have demonstrated the impact of Christian parenting and good study habits.

Because of the poverty and rapid spread of HIV/AIDS among the Suba people, many children are left orphaned. Naphtaly and Nereah established a Christian boarding school on Mfangano Island in 2003 called Gethsemane Garden Christian Centre, where Naphtaly is known as "Daddy." Starting with K-3, each year the school has added another grade and about forty more students. It numbered around 500 in 2011. The selection of Christian teachers has been crucial, and the children not only have found the love and security that they need, but the majority have found a heavenly Father who has purchased their right to be children of God.

Gethsemane Garden Christian Centre has become the most sought-after school where other families can pay to send their children. (The GGCC charter states that 80 percent of the students must be orphans.) Academically it has reached the highest level in the district, and the exemplary behavior of the students, even when they return to home villages during school breaks, has been a tremendous witness that they are Christ followers.

1 The total population of the Suba-speaking people is 90,000; 25,000 of those life on Mfangano Island. The language consists of five mutually intelligible dialects.

Chapter 17

The Woman That Cops Love To Hug!

Janet Hughlett

> God delights to use an ordinary person to do what no person could do alone! —*Anonymous*

Janet Hughlett is just an ordinary housewife in many ways. But this ordinary woman *is* extraordinary because of her fulfilling the vision the Lord gave her many years ago. And police officers in Pasco, Washington, and surrounding areas love to hug her!

She and her husband, John, attend Faith Assembly Christian Center in Pasco, which is famous in that area for their Adopt-a-Cop Program.[1] And that is the "vision" the Lord gave Janet—an outreach program to police officers.

Janet says, "In June 1995, we began praying for the sheriff and twenty-three deputies of Franklin County. Later that year we added three office personnel to our prayer list.

"The main things the Adopt-a-Cop Program includes are prayer and encouragement. Prayer for safety is a major item included in those prayers. Stress among police officers—particularly traumatic stress following injury, injuring others in the line of duty, or witnessing the death or injuries of other officers and civilians—has long concerned police managers, police union, and the friends and families of police officers.

"A law enforcement officer is killed in the line of duty every fifty-three hours. Every twenty-four to fifty-two hours a police officer commits suicide.[2] At the present time we are praying for 215 officers.[3] We have seen God do many wonderful things for the officers whom we 'adopt,'" Janet says.

In July 1998, the "Kids Adopt-a-Cop" ministry was established. "The children are extremely excited and write a note or draw a picture for 'their' officer.

"The goal God has given me is to first spread the word about Adopt-a-Cop across the nation so all law enforcement officers will have someone from their local community praying and writing them notes of encouragement.

"Each May during National Law Enforcement Week, we ask the women of our church to bake four dozen cookies each. Then volunteers put the cookies on trays for each agency that is on Adopt-a-Cop. For example, for Pasco Police, we have a tray for the day shift, the swing shift, and the graveyard shift, as well as the administration and office staff. We put a card on each tray indicating who it is for and a note that says:

'With our thanks and appreciation for your service to our community. Your friends at Faith Assembly Christian Center.'

"We deliver about 1,500 cookies. The officers always look forward to this time of year and the cookies they receive."

In 2004 John and Janet were part of a team that ministered to law enforcement officers in Cape Town, South Africa, for a couple weeks. One of the officers they met there gave Janet the following poem:

The Officer
I have been where you fear to be
I have seen what you fear to see
I have done what you fear to do
All these things I have done for you.

I am the person you lean upon
The one you cast your scorn upon
The one you bring your troubles to
All these people I've been for you.

The one you ask to stand apart
The one you feel should have no heart
The one you call in brown or blue
But I'm a person, just like you.

And through the years I've come to see
That I am not always what you ask of me.
So take this badge, take this gun
Will you take?...Will anyone?

And when you watch a person die,
And hear a battered baby cry,
Then do you think that you can be
All these things you ask of me?

Ten law enforcement officers attend our church on a regular basis. We are always adding new officers to our list as we offer words of encouragement and prayer support, depending on God to answer our prayers for them.

"In June 1995, we started praying for the sheriff and twenty-three deputies of Franklin County. Later that year we added three office personnel to our prayer list."

More about Janet Hughlett:

Janet and her husband, John, live in Pasco, Washington. John does freelance construction work, as well as gives advice about health tips to his friends via the computer. And Janet is still busy ministering to the "cops" and receiving hugs from them!

John and Janet have two children, Bill and Kathryn. Bill is married to Casie and they have two children, Jonathan and Janie. Kathryn, and her husband, Robert Maunton, have a daughter—Lauren Cleary. Carol, their first daughter, who has retained her maiden name, has two boys, Will and Wyatt.

1 Goals of Adopt-a-Cop: Daily cover the officers with prayer that God's protection will be around them and their families.

Pray for our community that we have a safe and peaceful place to live. Encourage the officers and let them know they are appreciated. Spread the word and see an "Adopt-a-Cop" program in cities all across America—and even in other countries.

2 The exact number of suicides varies from year to year. But it is generally thought that police officers commit suicide at a much higher rate than the general public. Police officers are also more likely to take their own lives than to be killed in the line of duty.

3 These officers serve in Franklin County Sheriff's Department, Benton County Sheriff's Department, Pasco Police, Kennewick Police, the Kennewick Detachment of the Washington State Patrol, some Pasco Airport Police, and Hanford Patrol, as well as some corrections officers from the Benton and Franklin County Jails.

Chapter 18

"Counterfeit Brown Paper?"

Jim Wilson

Turn your face to the sun [Son] and the shadows fall behind you. —Jan Goldstein, in *Sacred Wounds*

One day, over thirty-five years ago, Michael,[1] a college student, came into The Lamplighter,[2] a bookstore at the University of Maryland. He wandered around a bit, then introduced himself to Jim Wilson, the owner of the store, and decided to tell him why he was not a Christian.

"I'm not a Christian for two reasons. The first—because of the terrible things the Conquistadors, Crusaders, and Inquisitors did; and the second—because of the hypocrites in the church."

"I agree with you that those groups did 'terrible things,' and yes, there are hypocrites in the church. But I am a Christian. So I don't see the connection," said Jim.

The look on his face seemed to say, *You obviously didn't hear what I said! If you had, you'd understand!*

"Tell me, Michael, were the Conquistadors Christians?" Jim asked.

"Are you kidding? Of course you know they weren't Christians."

"Were the Crusaders Christians?"

"What are you leading up to? No, of course, they weren't!"

"Were the Inquisitors Christians?"

This time Michael simply answered, "No, they weren't Christians!"

"And what about those hypocrites in the church? Are—?"

Michael answered before Jim could finish his question. "No, they aren't Christians."

"That's interesting. You just told me that you're not a Christian because of four kinds of people you consider to be non-Christians. That doesn't make sense at all. That's like rejecting concrete because Styrofoam doesn't act like concrete. Tell me, have you heard of a counterfeit ten-dollar bill?"

"Sure. We all have."

"Why do people counterfeit ten-dollar bills?"

"The answer to that is obvious. It's because the real ten-dollar bill is worth ten dollars, and the counterfeit is worth nothing," Michael answered.

"Have you ever heard of counterfeit brown paper?"

"Counterfeit brown paper? Of course not."

"Well, why don't people make counterfeit brown paper?"

"The answer to that is simple: it's not worth anything."

"So you're saying there has to be a 'real' that's worth something before anyone will counterfeit it. Suppose you were cheated out of twenty dollars by exchanging a good twenty-dollar bill for two counterfeit ten-dollar bills. You'd get angry, wouldn't you? Would that make you reject US currency from then on? I reckon that would be foolish if you did! The fact that there is fake money out there proves that the real is worth something. Seeing counterfeit Christians should make you know that real Christians are out there. Hypocrites are like counterfeit ten-dollar bills."

"Hmmm, I never thought of it like that," Michael responded.

"Can I give you some advice, Michael?" Jim asked.

Michael grinned. "Sure. Go on…"

"Find a real Christian, one who's filled with love, joy, peace, and patience, and who clearly confesses the Lord Jesus Christ. Examine him, and then if you wish to reject Christianity because of the real, I'd say you're at least honest—even if not very smart. Or better yet, Michael, examine Jesus—the ultimate real—and reject Him. By the way, Michael, I'm speaking at an InterVarsity meeting later this evening over in the Student Union Building…. Come join us."

That evening, about seventy-five students crowded into the long, narrow room. "When I stood up to speak, I saw Michael standing in a corner. After the closing prayer, I turned to go over to where he was but was detained by a couple of women asking questions. By the time I'd finished answering their questions, Michael had disappeared."

But by the time Jim got to the door, Michael was there. "I thought you'd gone, Michael," he said.

"I did. I got out of there as fast as I could. I was at the other end of the building when two women students walked by. I heard one of them say, 'Too bad that fella Mr. Wilson invited left.' I figured they were talking about me, so I came back."

"Michael, if you want to talk, I'll listen," Jim said.

"No, you talk and I'll listen," Michael replied.

Back in the room, as Jim talked to him, Michael began to shake. Jim invited him to receive Jesus Christ.

Michael became defensive. "That's a personal thing!"

"That's right, Michael. It is. When you receive Christ, call the Lamplighter. In the meantime…good night."

"What do you mean?"

"It's late and I'm going home."

As Jim walked to his car, he heard someone call, "I couldn't make it back to my room. I have to receive Christ now."

And there in the parking lot, Jim led Michael to Jesus!

***More about Jim Wilson*:**

In 1968 he helped open an InterVarsity store in Ann Arbor, Michigan—Logos Bookstore. Jim opened the Christian Bookshop in Annapolis (OCF) in November of 1958, and The Lamplighter in College Park, Maryland (Christian Books in Annapolis) in 1968.

He was with InterVarsity only a year. There were at one time about eighty Logos Bookstores, most of which have closed. In 1971 Jim and his family went to Moscow, Idaho, with Community Christian Ministries.

In the next years he opened eight stores next to colleges or universities; five are still open, two of which he gave to local ministries. The remaining three are the Brushfire in Gunnison, Colorado; Oasis Books in Logan, Utah; and the NUART Theatre in Moscow, Idaho. The three schools are Western State College, Utah State University, and the University of Idaho.

Jim served in the Korean War from 1950 to 1953. In November 1950, he met Bessie in Yokohama where she was serving as headmistress of a girls' school. They were married in April 1952. Bessie is now with the Lord.

1 Michael is a pseudonym. Jim has lost contact with this man. We invite you to pray for Michael. Ask God to use him and give him joy and peace if he is still alive.

2 In 1963 Jim opened The Lamplighter in College Park, Maryland, to minister to students at the nearby University of Maryland.

Chapter 19

"Just a Computer"

The BTL Library Computer as told to the human, Aretta Loving

Submit to the Lord.... Serve the Lord your God (2 Chronicles 30:8).

"Any interesting stories regarding this project that perhaps indicate the Lord's blessing?" was the question asked on a Project Report Form. "This project" the form talks about is me, the BTL[1] Library computer. Would you believe it, the human filling in that form almost said no!

But he decided to let me talk for myself. And I say—and there is no "perhaps" about it—the Lord is making me a blessing to these humans involved in getting God's Word to the smaller language groups here in Kenya.

I and others like me support the entire effort of Bible translation in a fast-growing, worldwide network! Wycliffe Bible Translation uses state-of-the art programs for accounting, information management, and communication, as well as Bible translation.

I can tell you one thing—I don't have much time to get lonely or bored. Hardly a day goes by, except Sunday, that there isn't some human needing my help. In fact, often I'm awakened before seven in the morning and not allowed to rest again till after six in the evening. Usually I have the evenings to myself. But not always.

Ian Mowatt—he's from Scotland and works with BTL as the technical studies department manager—late last year, did a survey of the Turkana and Pokot languages of Kenya. The purpose of the survey was to determine the literacy needs there. In plain language, that means—Well, I interrupt myself to say that I don't see why these humans always want to make things so complicated! They think I'm complicated, but I'm really just a computer....

Well, as I was saying, in plain language that means they wanted to find out if those Turkana and Pokot humans were reading the Bible that has been translated into their languages. If they aren't, BTL wants to know how they can help them. Ian spent many long days with me, days that stretched into weeks, making a report of that survey. I'm just a computer, but I had a part in that.

Aretta Loving[2] is another human who spends quite a bit of time with me. She and her husband are Americans. Aretta is editor of *The Call of Kenya*, the BTL newsletter that goes out to Christians in Kenya. One issue had as the theme "Translation: A Team Effort." Those humans who gave money for BTL to buy me sure are a part of our team here in Kenya! Like Edwyn Kiptinness, a BTL board member, wrote in the September/October 1988 issue of *The Call of Kenya*:

> We are people of many nationalities, yet we are fighting and working to reach the same goal. Relating to each other and cooperating with each other is an important factor in reaching that goal. The task of translating the Word of God can only be tackled by working together.

Heli Voipio, the BTL librarian, is from Finland. You see, just like Edwyn said, these humans are from many different countries. But they all have this in common: they love God and they work together in Bible translation in order that people's hearts and minds might be enlightened by the Light of the world. Heli writes letters ordering linguistic books and magazines. (These books and magazines are to help those humans who are learning and analyzing the languages of those where they work.)

Heli's husband is a computer expert. That means he knows how to fix me. I like him. So do these humans, because they get awfully upset when something goes wrong with me.

I guess they like me too even though I'm just a computer. I don't get to go out to the villages and have Scripture typed on me, as some of those little battery-operated computers get to. I'm just a library computer, but I have a big part in giving the Light to people here in Kenya. Someone has said that God allowed computers to be invented to speed up Bible translation, and He lets others use us. How sad that some people use us for bad things. But those humans who work with *me* are thankful for me and they always use me for good things!

And they're awfully thankful to those humans who gave money for "this project." That's me—just a computer, the BTL library computer. But I have yielded myself to serve God, just as 2 Chronicles tells us to.

But I want you to remember that hard drives in hot places tend to react irrationally. When we go down, who is there to cheer us up?

Why don't you join Wycliffe and be a computer cheerer-upper?

1 Bible Translation and Literacy organization, East Africa.

2 Aretta Loving served as editor for BTL while she and Ed were working under BTL for a four-year period.

Chapter 20

Encircled by a Halo

Mike Mower, about Shirley Baum

God longs to fill our land with glory
So that His righteousness may be seen by all.
He will fill our hearts with refreshing springs
If today we will listen to His call.
—*Anonymous*

Leaning out of the small, single-engine plane, Shirley threw out exactly six boxes, one by one, just as I had instructed her. She smiled as she watched each one land in the large clearing between the two mountains.

Seven years before, at age sixty-four, Shirley had joined Wycliffe and gone to the Philippines to help with Bible translation any way she could. She was assigned to the Nasuli Center on the island of Mindanao. Each morning, for exercise, she walked along the airstrip and prayed,

> Lord, thank You for Your creation. Thank You that You've given me the privilege of serving You in these beautiful surroundings. I love the orchids and flame trees. And Mount Capistrano—I never tire of seeing that gorgeous view.

As Shirley threw out those boxes, she thought, *What a welcome break from my secretarial work. And it's fun to see how mail and cargo that I package for our translators are delivered.*

The afternoon before, as the Center pilot, I had telephoned Shirley and told her we had received a radio message from a New Tribes Mission couple living in a remote village. "They don't have an airstrip and need supplies delivered by an air drop flight. Would you be willing to help as the 'dropper' for that flight tomorrow morning?" I asked her.

Shirley certainly was willing—more than willing. She was delighted!

Shirley had commented earlier, "It pleases me to know that our pilots serve other missions as well as our own translators by delivering building materials, medical supplies, mail, groceries—and sometimes even floating down eggs on a special little parachute."

She arrived at the hanger at 5 a.m. and confessed that she had "a restless night thinking about the exciting day ahead." She watched as the right door of the small aircraft was taken off and listened intently as I gave her instructions about how to perform the tasks of dropper. Then she climbed into the seat and buckled up. I wrapped a thin piece of tape around the seat belt buckle to help prevent it from accidentally opening. Then I added a second seat belt, connected to the lower seat structure, around Shirley's left leg. I then taxied out and we took off from Nasuli's grass runway.

When relating her experience, Shirley said, "After about twenty-five minutes, just as my feelings of trepidation had changed to anticipation, it was time for Mike to set the plane down on another small airstrip where New Tribes had their headquarters. There thirty boxes were loaded onto the small plane.

"Taking off again, another thirty minutes of flight offered an unexcelled view of large rainforests interspersed with lakes. Then up over a mountain we headed to our destination: a clearing between two mountains. Mike flew one trip around the drop pattern, and people began running out of their houses waving up at us. On the next pass I pulled one of the boxes onto my lap and at Mike's command, '*DROP!*' I leaned out and dropped the first box. I began to almost feel like an old pro at this throwing-out-boxes bit, when on the fourth pass, my elbow hit my seat belt and unlocked it. I tried to relock it but was not successful. *Well, what can I do but keep throwing out these last boxes?* I thought."

"Shirley, wave at the people, so they'll know we're finished," I instructed.

"After I waved at the people, I once again tried to fasten my seat belt—this time, *click!* It was locked," Shirley relates.

Hearing that *click*, I turned toward her. "Shirley, don't take off your seat belt. That could be extremely dangerous with no door on the plane," I told her.

"'I haven't taken off my seat belt,,' Shirley replied. 'I'll explain later.' Mike gave me a 'What-was-that-noise?' look and then glanced down at my seat belt. Satisfied that it was fastened, he pointed to a cloud. 'Look over there. That's called "the glory." I looked and was delighted to see a circular rainbow with the airplane's shadow exactly in the middle!

"Later when I explained to Mike about what had happened to my seat belt, he told me that without the second seat belt I could have fallen out of the plane during the moderately steep turns in the drop pattern. Hearing that, I knew that reflection of our plane encircled by a halo had been a message from God. I felt He said, *Shirley, I protected you today. And I will protect you into your old age.*

Thank You, Lord, that You have many more years for me to serve You, I whispered in my spirit.

And God was faithful to give Shirley many more years of service for him. At eighty-five, Shirley was still using her secretarial skills, not in the Philippines, but at JAARS, Wycliffe's technical support center in North Carolina—still doing what God had equipped her to do in order to further the work of Bible translation.

After going into a retirement home at age ninety, recently she went to be with the Lord. *Those planted in the house of the LORD…will flourish in the courts of our God. They will still bear fruit in old age…* (Psalm 92:12–13).

***More about Mike Moyer*:**

Mike and his wife, Pat, served in the Philippines for nearly twenty years and are now assigned to the JAARS Center in North Carolina. Both work in the Missions at the Airport program, a public relations outreach of JAARS. Through Missions at the Airport they are sharing the story of JAARS and the needs of the Bible-less peoples with churches, schools, camps, and conference centers around the country.

Mike and Pat's two children grew up in the Philippines. Joshua was 3½ years old and Elizabeth was six months old when they first arrived in that country. Joshua, a nuclear technician on submarines in the US Navy, was taken home to be with the Lord at age twenty-three. Elizabeth lives and works in the Charlotte, North Carolina, area as an accountant.

Chapter 21

The Power of Blessing

Aretta Loving, about Maki

All they [the disciples] could see were black skies as they bounced in the battered boat.
Then a figure came to them walking on the water. It wasn't what they expected....
They almost missed seeing the answer to their prayers.
And unless we look and listen clearly, we risk making the same mistake.
God's light in our dark nights are as numerous as the stars, if only we'll look for them.
—*Max Lucado*[1]

"He's dying! My brother's dying!" a very distraught Konime told us.

Konime, a pastor in Papua New Guinea, was near tears as he related the condition of his brother. He was convinced that his brother, Maki, would die because "someone put a curse on him." As far as Konime was concerned, absolutely nothing he or anyone else could do for his brother now would make a difference.

Still he had come to us with his concern. "Come with me and pray with me for my brother. He's dying!"

We stooped and entered Maki's dark hut, and there we found him lying on his sleeping mat, unable to walk and barely able to speak.

"He won't eat the food I bring him," his wife tearfully confided to us.

"It's true. He is dying. And he will die unless God intervenes," both Ed and I concluded.

"Maki, we've come here to pray for you. Is it all right if we do that?" Ed asked. A slight nod of his head conveyed his yes.

We sensed that we were representatives of the body of Christ in that place, at that time. We laid our hands on him and prayed. "Father God, we come to You, the One who rules over all creation in heaven and earth. Fill Your servants with Your Holy Spirit."

We cried out to our heavenly Father, interceding for Him to intervene for Maki. *This man is in need of Your mercy and grace….*

We spoke forth the Word:

> *I have set before you life and death, blessings and curses. Now choose life, so that you and your children may live and that you may love the Lord your God, listen to his voice, and hold fast to him. For the Lord is your life…* (Deuteronomy 30:19–20).

We chose life and blessing for Maki. *…and Lord, cause him to also choose life over death, Your blessing over the enemy's curse.* We spoke a blessing over Maki. *Lord, we know You want to bless Your child Maki. And we bless him.*

Last of all, we rebuked the curse. *In the all-powerful name of Jesus, we say No! to this curse.*

Finally, exhausted and feeling the battle won, for some minutes we sat quietly in expectation of what God would do. We watched with thanksgiving to our miracle-working God as Maki sat up. Though still weak, he looked up at us and smiled. Before we left, his wife brought him food and he began to eat.

As we walked back home, the day was slipping into night and stars shone above us. But by faith we praised God that the darkness we found in Konime's hut and in Maki's life that day had left.

A literal hands-on experience that day taught us how exceedingly powerful a curse is. We also realized in contrast that if a curse is this powerful, how much more powerful is a blessing when given in the all-powerful name of Jesus Christ!

When Ed and I returned to Papua New Guinea to assist Faith Comes By Hearing[2] record the Awa New Testament, we met Maki's daughter and rejoiced as she told us Konime had baptized his brother a few months afterward.

1 *In the Eye of the Storm,* 1991, Thomas Nelson Publishers

2 The mission of Hosanna/Faith Comes By Hearing (FCBH) is based on the verses in Matthew 28:19–20: "go and make disciples of all nations, teaching them to obey everything the Lord has commanded." In order to do this, they provide, free of charge, the audio New Testament to language groups in their heart language, the language they pray in. Over half the people in the world today cannot read and have no means of understanding the written Word of God. By recording the New Testament in audio form, FCBH provides a solution to this problem and furthers the Great Commission. They then provide a free copy of that recording to every church or churches in that language group. Each group then commits to gather weekly to listen through the New Testament and discuss it. Thus FCBH endeavors to bring His church together and make disciples from every nation, tribe, language, and people. *So then faith comes by hearing, and hearing by the word of God* (Romans 10:17 NKJV). FCBH produced a recording of the Awa language for use in PNG. "We share the Lovings' concern for those older people who cannot read," says Bob Sharpe in Tijunga, California. Jerry Jackson is the founder and president of FCBH.

Chapter 22

"I Will Follow"

Wolfgang Baumruck

This is what the Lord says—your Redeemer, the Holy One of Israel: "I am the Lord your God, who teaches you what is best for you, who directs you in the way you should go" (Isaiah 48:17).

Wolfgang grew up in a traditional, religious German family and was taken to church every Sunday by his parents.

"As a small boy, my ears stuck straight out, and because of that my classmates at school made fun of me. And my ears still do stick out but fortunately it's not as noticeable now—or maybe I'm less concerned about what people think I look like!

"Our area of Germany was famous for flying gliders—and that's what my classmates called me—Glider. Being made fun of and called Glider destroyed my self-confidence."

In the area where Wolfgang lived, he saw helicopters from the US military flying overhead, and it always excited him. At a young age, he decided, *When I grow up, I want to become a helicopter pilot.* He loved the feeling of seeing the choppers in flight!

Wolfgang had one brother, Uwe, born a year before he was. "We were known as 'The Baumies'—and I was tagged as 'The Little Baumie.' Uwe's friends called me that, sometimes with a condescending tone of voice, as though I was a second-class person.

"After I became an adult, I wanted to show everybody that I was *more* than a second-class person. I was not a nobody—but a 'somebody. *And by becoming a helicopter pilot, I can do that,*" I decided.

"God, in His mercy, granted me my desire, even though at that time I hadn't come to faith in Jesus Christ. I joined the German Army and was transferred to the United States for flight training.

"And along with me was a German friend who told me about his faith in Jesus Christ. When I was a child and going to our traditional church, I went to communion classes on a regular basis. For my faithful attendance, the priest gave me a Good News Bible. I read it but only once in a while. Reading about the penalty of sin caused me to have a stomachache. So I put the Bible away.

"But when my military friend gave me his testimony of faith in Jesus Christ, I knew what he was talking about, and God's Spirit had made me know that it *was* indeed true. So I was faced with the challenge: *Do I go in this direction or not?* I didn't want to be converted by my friend because I was just becoming a helicopter pilot and kind of riding on cloud nine!"

Wolfgang avoided his friend whenever possible. But he decided to visit different churches to find out for himself what they were like. "And," he says, "I saw that some churches were alive with the Holy Spirit and the Light of God that presented to me the truth of God and His Word. But in other churches I couldn't see life. I finally decided to go with my friend to the church where he went.

"And there, at age twenty-two, in December 1986, after hearing the truth preached for a number of Sundays, I gave my life to Jesus Christ.

"Then when I went back to Germany, I decided to stay in the military and become a career soldier. It was a good job and it was fun flying a helicopter. Soon I met several other Christians in a military Bible study group who had joined the military to get the training necessary to become missionary aviators. Again this thought excited me.

"The thought of becoming a missionary aviator came back again and again. I didn't have peace about staying in the military to serve for the rest of my life without being able to get out. That seemed like bondage to me. In the meantime I had come to know my wife—Damaris."

A Christian flight instructor at the German Army Aviation School facilitated a military Bible study that Wolfgang joined. This flight instructor was an elder at a local church. He also led this church's youth group. His church had grown and they had built a larger building in which to meet. They invited guests to come to the dedication of the building.

On this guest list was Wolfgang's would-be father-in-law who had moved to a different city to minister—and that city was Wolfgang's home town. At the dedication, Wolfgang met his future wife's mother and was very impressed with her. Later that day he met Damaris, and he was very, very impressed with her, as she was with him!

"After Damaris and I were married, we started looking into mission organizations. Finally I withdrew my application to become a career soldier and began to go in the direction of mission aviation.

"I had signed a nine-year contract with the military, so I had to finish those nine years. During that time God provided the opportunity for training as an aircraft maintenance technician—training that was needed to upgrade and maintain missionary aircraft.

"Also I enrolled in a one-year Brethren Bible School program, called Wiedenest, to get the necessary theological training to be able to serve in missions.

"Later we were accepted by a mission, and our family came to the United States. By then we had two small children. In the States I was accepted by Moody Aviation for a one-year aircraft mechanic training program. In the following year I acquired the necessary US commercial helicopter and airplane licenses to be able to join Missionary Aviation Fellowship (MAF) to fly their helicopters.

"After that we were accepted by MAF and went back to Germany for deputation. Within a short time—four months—we had all the financial support we needed to serve overseas. So in 1998 we were transferred to language school in Bandung on the island of Java. And a year later we were in Irian Jaya, serving with MAF. We served a total of thirteen years in Irian Jaya (now known as Papua, Indonesia), to the west of Papua New Guinea.

"Our two daughters grew up in Indonesia and both attended an international school there, speaking English most of the day. Our first daughter, Frauke, born in 1990, wanted to attend a US college but could not do so for lack of finances. So she went back to Germany and began an apprenticeship.

"Svenka, born in 1992, finished international school just recently in 2011. She too wanted to come to the US for college. By then we had found an affordable Christian college, and we thought as parents it would be good to accompany her and be available in this new important stage of her life. So we were given permission from our mission to come to the United States and work as volunteers at JAARS, Wycliffe's support center and aviation arm in Waxhaw, North Carolina.

"Here at JAARS I started the much desired and needed self-education. Each day I study aviation safety management, which I hope I can use in the future to make missionary aviation safer.

"We don't know where God will lead us, but our desire is to serve the Lord Jesus as a family. And we are confident that He will lead us! And we do affirm that 'where He leads us, we will follow. And what He feeds us we will swallow'—and that includes even ground beef and fast foods!" And when Wolfgang says that he thinks of a sign posted in a Bible school cafeteria that says:

> Where He leads me, I will follow.
> What He feeds me, I will swallow.

But even so, when he has to eat ground beef or any fast foods, his face shows exactly how he feels about these!

***More about Wolfgang Baumnuck*:**

Wolfgang's parents, Friedrich and Elisabeth Baumruck, live in Fulda, Germany. His father-in-law went to be with the Lord in 1997, and his mother-in-law lives in Fulda, as well.

Wolfgang and Damaris are currently residing at the JAARS Center in Waxhaw, North Carolina. Wolfgang continues his studies as they listen to the Lord for His next direction for them.

Chapter 23

"Silent Night" United Common Enemies

Phillip Gregory

Silent night, holy night, all is calm, all is bright round yon virgin mother and child.
Holy infant, so tender and mild, sleep in heavenly peace, sleep in heavenly peace.

Stille Nacht, heilige Nicht! Alles schlaft, einsam wacht mudas traulehoch heilige Paar,
Holder Knabe mit locigem Haar, schalf im himmlischer Ruh, schlaf im himmlischer Ruh.

"In 1977 when I was serving with a full bird colonel from England during training exercises in Grafenwoehr, Germany, we were sitting around a campfire. Since it was late November, talk from the Americans revolved around Thanksgiving. The old colonel spoke up when the time was right. He told of his grandfather's story about the winter of 1914," Phillip says.

"As Christmas approached," the colonel said, "the young British soldiers were homesick. They gathered what special food they could in an attempt to celebrate Christmas Eve. Apparently, the Germans who held the ground across from the entrenched British had the same feelings. As the magic hour approached, all shooting ceased. In the stillness and silence, a lone voice rose from across the no-man's land. *Stille Nacht*, what the British knew as the song 'Silent Night,' came drifting across the wilderness. One by one, the Brits joined in. Soon hundreds of voices came together in a mix of German and English, singing the beloved song. Then from across the frozen ground came a voice in broken English, 'Hey, soldier, you want some German brown bread?' And it was answered by a scared British voice asking, 'Hey, Hymie, you want some British tea?' "

The German soldier stood up, slowly at first. After no shots rang out, he stood a bit taller. A lone British soldier also stood up, fearing a German bullet. Not one shot came. The two soldiers walked toward each other, having to step gingerly across the destroyed landscape. They met halfway, exchanging their gifts. They wished each other a merry Christmas and returned to their comrades. Once again, the song rose up. The soldiers joined in as midnight arrived.

The next morning, the German soldier rose up from his bunker. The British soldier rose to meet him. As they began to walk toward each other, other soldiers from each side joined in. Bread, cake, beer, tea, and other goodies were exchanged. One of the officers suggested that they move over to an area that was not so damaged by the war. As they did, one of the Brits threw out a "soccer" ball. A game of "football" (soccer) began that lasted until nearly noon. As more officers from both sides arrived, it was decided that it might not be a good idea to continue this unofficial armistice. Each side went back to their trenches. Later that afternoon, the war resumed.

The colonel said that until the day he died, his grandfather told the story of his comrades singing "Silent Night" across the forbidden land with German soldiers who were also missing their homes. Many older soldiers in the Seventh Army had served with Patton and others in the last days of World War II. They had also served during an extremely harsh winter in 1944 with members of the 101st Airborne Division at a place called Bastogne, Belgium. They had been holed up as shells rained down all around. On Christmas Eve, around 9 p.m., all shelling stopped. The snow dampened the sound and made for a memorable evening. A bit later, a voice began singing "Silent Night." Soon others joined in. Germans and Americans joined in singing the well-known ballad for over an hour. For this brief period of time, there was no war. "Silent Night" united common enemies for a brief time, which brought the war to a standstill.

"I heard many stories of the war in Korea," Phillip says. "We never referred to Korea as a 'conflict.' It was always referred to as a 'war' by those who served. I must have heard a thousand times of the extreme temperatures in Korea. Those who had served during the entire war said that it was the coldest conditions they had ever endured. I heard stories of coffee freezing solid in canteen cups, moments after having been served. There were stories of discovering North Korean and Chinese soldiers frozen solid on patrol."

As Christmas approached in 1950, many American soldiers could not believe that they were back at war. A large number had been released after their service in World War II, only to be recalled five years later. Here they were, serving in a land quite unlike where they had fought in only a short five years earlier. They were homesick. They were cold. They were thousands of miles from the United States.

On Christmas Eve, in an area known as Chanju, a number of these soldiers were gathered in an attempt to stay warm, heat up something to drink, and celebrate as best they could. In the stillness, one of the soldiers asked the others if they had just heard what he had heard. As they all quieted down, singing could be heard coming from across the way. The words were in Korean, but the melody was well known—"Silent Night"! The Americans joined in. For many, it was the first time that North Korean soldiers had been allowed that close. It was unsettling. Suddenly, one of the Americans shouted out, "Halt. Who goes there?" Three North Korean soldiers came slowly walking up the little dirt road. They held their rifles up over their heads. When they were around thirty yards away, they stopped. One of them spoke up, "Merry Christmas, GI."

"Merry Christmas," one of the Americans shouted back, and then a North Korean set a parka on the ground. Slowly the North Koreans backed away. The American sergeant told one of the young privates to slowly see what had been left.

Carefully, the soldier made his way to the parka, making sure that it was not rigged to explode. He then turned back to the sergeant and explained that under the parka were cookies, Korean beer, and canned meat. He brought the gifts back to the Americans. Quickly, the GIs gathered up a feast and returned it to the parka as a return gift. Then from across the woods came the voice of a North Korean soldier. "Merry Christmas, GI." And the Americans returned the greeting. Another chorus of "Silent Night" followed. Soon, both groups were safely back in their lines. It was the Christmas of 1950 in a land far away.

"While I served with the Department of Defense in Europe, one of my assignments was to pull duty on the border near Hof, Germany. We had observation posts strategically located all along the border. The East Germans and Soviets also had their observation posts placed along the border. More often than not, they were quite close, separated by strands of barbed wire and a simple dirt road that was constantly raked in order to make sure that footprints could be easily seen. We watched them; they watched us. We also regularly monitored radio transmissions. In addition to regular army personnel, each side had intelligence personnel assigned to each post. We were ordered to report on each duty assignment as to incidents and anything else that might be pertinent to the security of the border.

"On Christmas Eve of 1978, I was standing in my observation post with two other American soldiers. It was a simple ten-foot-square structure that sat thirty feet off the ground. We had 180 degrees of visibility through bulletproof glass. A walkway went all around the three sides facing East Germany. We had high-powered binoculars through which we constantly watched our counterparts across the dividing line. My binoculars gave me outstanding visibility of my counterpart. I could tell if he was in a good mood. I could see whether he had shaved that morning. I could usually tell if he had clipped his nose hairs that week. The two of us seldom wore military clothing. We were allowed to wear civilian clothing unless we were on alert. We even had a space heater in the post.

"I had been assigned to this post for over two months. My counterpart and I usually served the same ten-hour shift. We knew each other, not by name, but because we constantly watched each other and our surroundings. We could never be friends, but we could be cordial. I always waved hello as I came on shift, and he always returned the gesture.

"Once again, it was Christmas Eve and it *was* cold! I put on my cold-weather overcoat and stepped out onto the walkway. My German counterpart did the same. He held up his coffee cup. I held up mine. From across the distance, I heard him begin to sing 'Silent Night.' My German was pretty good. I knew the story of 'Silent Night,' and I knew the love the Germans had for the story and the melody. I joined in.

"My two enlisted men came out of the post and asked me what the heck was going on. My counterpart's two military men came out, and I suppose that they asked him the same thing. Soon, all six of us were singing 'Silent Night.' At the conclusion of several verses, my German counterpart held up his coffee cup. I held up mine. Then all six of us walked back into our respective posts. I looked over and could see that he had put down his binoculars and was sitting with his friends. I put down my pair of binoculars and sat down with my friends. We drank hot coffee and ate cookies. For the remainder of the night, there was no monitoring of Soviet or German activities from across Monitoring Post 17 on the border. They could have driven a whole division of Soviet tanks across the border on Christmas Eve in 1978.

"In my morning report, I indicated that nothing had occurred. As far as the official report is concerned, all was quiet on the border of the two Germanys. 'Silent Night' had—once again—put an end to hatred and the Cold War, at least for a brief time, and united common enemies.

"I often wonder how my counterpart remembers that night. Does he tell his children and his children's children how he and his American friend decided to stop the foolishness for a brief spell one Christmas Eve, and celebrated Christmas over coffee and cookies, far from home?"

***More about Phillip Gregory*:**

Captain Phillip Gregory spent a number of years assigned to the Seventh Army, Europe, in his early days with the United States government. Many older soldiers who had served in the latter days of World War II, Korea, and Vietnam were still on active duty. Phillip held a position that afforded him the opportunity to be involved both with officers and enlisted men on a daily basis. Their stories of their time overseas provided a wealth of information on men serving under stressful conditions in lands far from home.

Chapter 24

A Most Inconvenient Christmas

Leah Ruth Blauser

> You could take all the Christmas trees ever lit, all the man-made lights of all ages; the lights of Creation—the sun, moon and stars—but all these would never match the glorious light of Jesus. —*Dr. Donnie Gamble*

"Mom wanted to go to Pennsylvania for Christmas. People at church assured me that they would be praying for us as we traveled."

So Leah Ruth drove her mother to Pennsylvania on Thursday.

"I got up at 3 a.m. Friday morning, and as soon as I was ready, headed out for home. Since it was close to Christmas I had my Christmas CDs in the car. As I drove south I looked out my window toward the east and there was a huge star there. *Wow!* I said to myself. *That's so big that I figure it has to be a planet!* I was later told it was probably Venus. That 'star' stayed right beside me as I drove through the early morning—which really was night because it was still quite dark.

"As I drove and saw the light of that beautiful star shining down on me, I prayed, *Lord, I know that many people have prayed and are praying for me as I travel. And I know that You are with me all the time. But I do thank You for that bright, beautiful reminder of that fact."*

A lot of the Christmas songs Leah Ruth listened to were about "the star," which made her feel even more that "her star" was a gift from God to guide her safely home. For quite a while after daylight had broken and all the other stars had disappeared, that one star kept shining.

"As I drove along with the comfort of that star and my CD playing, I was startled to hear words from Kyle Matthew's song 'The Most Inconvenient Christmas.' The first verse tells about bills received with a postcard offering apologies that the Christmas gifts 'you've ordered aren't in stock.'

"Those words spoke to me…

"I had planned to buy sweatshirts and do crafting on them to take as gifts to Pennsylvania. And I had looked for the sweatshirts and the items needed to craft them all summer. I was not able to find an infant sweatshirt even remotely close to the right color in any of the stores I looked in.

"I even got Glenn involved—in November he checked on his computer and could only find white sweatshirts. 'Alright, order them. I'll dye them,' I told him. He ordered, but…none came. After unanswered e-mails and phone calls—I was about to panic!

"Then I remembered that long ago I had decided that the birth of our Lord is not about all of the stuff we do to make ourselves have a good time. I resolved that getting stressed over trying to make Christmas 'perfect' was defeating the purpose of Christmas."

Glenn ordered the sweatshirts on November 27th, and the items were to be delivered in three days by UPS. "We should have at least heard something from them! They billed us," I complained to Glenn.

"So, forgetting my resolve, another e-mail to the company—and I was slightly angry when I wrote it—I told those faceless and voiceless 'thems' that not getting the shirt or hearing from them was most inconvenient…

"After I sent that e-mail and prayed to calm my anger and keep true to the spirit of Christmas, I chuckled because the Lord put words of a song from my Oak Ridge Boys Christmas CD in my head. Funny that I had chosen the word *inconvenient*—the title to the song and actually to the whole album is "The Most Inconvenient Christmas" written by Kyle Matthews and sung by the Oak Ridge Boys. They sing about packing up the kids to go to Grandpa's house, encountering a blizzard and the car breaking down!

"I sent up a quick prayer to God asking that He keep my car running, before turning my attention back to the singing. The next words they sang were about "the most inconvenient Christmas ever"–that first Christmas when God came "so far." And the purpose for His coming: to offer Himself for us!

So when the rush of Christmas "hits" each December, in his song Matthews admonishes us to remember that "God is with us!"

"After praying and recalling these words with so much meaning couched in the silliness of the first two verses, even though I'm disappointed about the shirts, I know it's not the end of the world. I hope we all celebrate Christmas for what it truly is and not for the 'stuff.'

"I later learned that my mother-in-law had a lot of pain that night and couldn't sleep so she was praying for me."

***More about Leah Ruth Blauser*:**

Leah Ruth was born the youngest and only girl into a Christian family. Her father was extremely serious about soul winning, and he instilled that in her at an early age. Her mother taught her to persevere and show Christian love in rough times. Leah Ruth came to know Jesus as Savior on her fourth birthday. "I loved Him and have had a desire to live for Him ever since," she says.

She confesses that "as a young girl with a desire to be a wife and a mother, I began to look for a husband instead of just serving

God and letting Him bring a man into my life. I married a Christian, but I wanted God to bless my marriage without really seeking His face about the marriage."

They had a son—who, Leah Ruth says, "was the joy of my life. He was always pleasant and we had a great relationship…." But when he was twenty-one, his father and Leah Ruth ended their rocky twenty-two years of marriage. At that point her health was not good, which caused her financial situation to be unstable. Her son didn't handle the divorce well, and their relationship became almost non-existent. "My friends had moved on in their lives and I felt like everything that was important to me in life was gone. But I found I had everything I needed in Jesus, and no one could take that from me!

"God has blessed me with a dear Christian husband and daily shows me His wonderful love, grace, mercy, forgiveness, joy, faithfulness…. Though some things are still not what I want them to be, I have been able to rest in my loving God and live a blessed life. I strive to be a blessing to the God who has done so much for me."

Chapter 25

"I Got Something Better'n a Big Buck This Year!"

Mike Wallman

To learn to read is to light a fire; every syllable that is spelled out is a spark. —*Victor Hugo*

By 9 a.m., people drawn by the subject "What Am I Here For?" packed the church. Small groups would meet once a week and study Rick Warren's forty-day *Purpose Driven Life* program.

Mike, one of the attendants, became a Christian when he was twenty years old. He married a Christian young woman, only to lose her in a motorcycle accident two years later. Then he met and married Diane, another strong Christian. "But," Mike says, "I found it difficult to grow in my faith because I couldn't read and make sense of the words I read."

Despite that, Mike purchased a Rick Warren book. "I decided to not even try to read it. Rather I would get the messages from Pastor Peter's Sunday messages," Mike says.

In the midst of the study, hunting season began and Mike decided to go north for bow-hunting—all alone. Not knowing why he did so, he tossed Rick's book in his car. Each day for three rainy days with no deer in sight, he climbed up into his hunting blind.

"On Saturday, the weather cleared, and I saw a deer in the distance. I looked down at the deer, and the deer looked up at me. Suddenly a strange sensation swept over me. Instead of shooting the deer, I climbed down and walked back to my cabin. There I picked up Rick's book and read seven chapters, and I understood what I read—a miracle from God!"

Mike phoned Diane. "I'm coming home with a big surprise for you!" he told her.

Diane began to think of how they'd handle the deer that she just knew Mike would come home with. *It must be a really big one! I've not heard so much excitement from him in a long time,* she thought. Meeting him at the door, her first question was—"Where's the buck?"

"I got something better'n a big buck this year!"

"Well, come on inside and tell me," Diane replied.

Mike told it all, and they rejoiced together over his new God-given ability! "What a mighty God we serve!" Mike says.

> *And we once again realize that in Christ all the fullness of the Deity lives in bodily form, and you have been given fullness in Christ, who is the head over every power and authority* (Colossians 2:9–10).

More about Mike Wallman:

Mike now enjoys church so much more as he is able to follow Scripture reading with understanding. He works as a fireman and his wife, Diane, works part-time at their church, Faith Reformed. Mike and Diane were married in 1974 and have two children, Bryan and Brooke. Both are following the Lord.

Chapter 26

"Handle With Care!"

Aretta Loving, about Shokari

"I, the Lord, have called you in righteousness; I will take hold of your hand. I will keep you" (Isaiah 42:6).

"Fragile! Handle with Care!" We've all seen that stamped on a package. Have you, like me, ever wished you could stamp that on yourself for all—or at least those in your household—to see? Or maybe another stamp you've seen on items in a store: "Breakable. Do Not Touch!"

At times we all feel fragile, even breakable—and also like that package: dark inside. Some would call it "having a bad hair day." Others would call it "being down." The medical profession calls it depression. We might hope it can be blamed on some physical problem or on a genetic disposition to depression so we can take a pill and *presto!* Gone!

But it can be related to some spiritual cause with the result of being disciplined from the Lord. His discipline calls for confession and receiving God's forgiveness, which often can be harder than the pill solution because, at such times, we feel unworthy of God's love and forgiveness.

I remember one week when I was feeling fragile. *Hey, I'm*

booked to give a devotional to a group of women, and I'm having a "bad hair week," not just a "bad hair day." What can I say to them? I asked myself.

Fortunately, I've learned that it's not myself (at least it's not *supposed* to be myself) that I present but the One who conquered fragility, the One who gained victory over death—and bad hair days, weeks, and months—through all the years of my life here on earth and into eternity, where there will never again be bad hair days!

I had returned home from three nights of staying with my three grandsons while their mom went with their dad on an out-of-town business trip. A mother of three super-active sons needs a break, and ordinarily I enjoy those times when I can give her that break. But what about when I'm feeling "breakable" and all three grandsons are like kangaroos in an egg-packing plant?

I had a run-in with the fifteen-year-old at the breakfast table. He argued with me over something I asked him to do, then asked—or rather, demanded—"Why should I have to?"

I couldn't claim that he had to "because I am bigger than you!" because he was over six feet tall!

Our grandsons have been trained to submit to authority, so when I gave him that time-honored, wisdom-packed answer—"Because I said so!"—he immediately did what I said. He didn't do it too happily, but he did it.

Well, the incident didn't help my fragile feeling much. As I said the blessing for our food, I told the Lord—and thereby also my grandson—that I forgave him and asked God to help both of us.

Feeling fragile that morning brought to mind a small Awa child from Papua New Guinea who was indeed fragile. A sad little boy he was, always clothed in nothing more than sunshine and a scowl. Cross-eyed, knock-kneed, scaly-skinned, dirty—that was Sokari. He didn't come near our village house much. When he did, he mostly stood at a distance and watched Ed and me interact with the other Awa kids.

One day Sokari teamed up with Inauga, a precocious young "lady" about the same age as he was. They took bananas from our outside food-storage table. Wow! How it delighted the other kids to tattle on Sokari and Inauga. You would have thought they were identifying confirmed bank robbers.

How should I handle this? I couldn't let them think stealing was okay, despite the fact that a couple of bananas was no big deal, I reasoned.

"*Mahbeq seto, teawo!* (Tell them both to come)," I instructed one of the bigger boys. They came: Inauga, smiling, with an "I know you, Aretta-Old-Woman; your bark is worse than your bite" attitude; Sokari with an "I-don't-know-you-and-I'm-terrified!" look on his face.

First, I lectured the two budding young "robbers." I then lifted Inauga's tiny bark skirt and lightly swatted her bare bottom. The result—a smirk that said, "Is that all? Those bananas were well worth those three swats."

Then Sokari. No skirt, not even a G-string, to lift. Could I bring myself to swat his scaly little bottom—even lightly? I wondered. But he needed to know that stealing food was a "not-done-thing."

After I delivered his three swats, he stood in silence. Huge tears channeled their way around the scales on his cheeks, carrying rivulets of mud with them. I stifled the urge to take this sad little child in my arms and comfort him.

The next day as I stood talking to a group of people, I felt a small body press close to my leg and a foot placed on my foot. Not unusual. Awa kids often did that. It was their way of letting me know "I like you."

I looked down. Crossed eyes looked up at me, and a dirty, scaly-skinned face emitted a shy smile—a smile that lit up his face and make it look cleaner and not so scaly. I smiled back, then reached down and took his hand.

From that day onward, I could expect that if Sokari was around me, he would put a small, horny foot on top of my foot. He would stand and hold my hand as he pressed his bare body close to my leg.

I often think when I'm feeling fragile, *Oh Lord, let me be like Sokari! When I need Your discipline, may I accept it knowing You love me, knowing You always want the best for me. Then may I press close to You and smile up into Your face. You'll smile back at me, lighten my burdens—and reach down and take my hand.*

I'm so glad God always handles me with care! Yes, He promised, "I am always with you," and He holds me by my right hand (see Psalm 73:2). And I'm glad He smiles at me with love—His smile really "lights up my life."

More about Sokari:

Once when leaving the village by helicopter, we took Sokari with us to the Ukarumpa Center. The center clinic doctor prescribed an ointment to treat his condition. He stayed with an Awa couple who were living and working there, and he would come to our house each day for me to put the ointment on his skin.

When we returned to the village, he went back to the village and I continued to treat him. The next time we were away, he died. I believe someday I'll see that little boy "up there" with perfect skin.

Sokari probably had scleroderma, described on the internet as "a multisystem disorder characterized by inflammatory, vascular, and sclerotic changes of the skin and various internal organs, especially the lungs, heart, and GI tract. At present, there are no proven treatments or cure for scleroderma of any form."

Chapter 27

Who Is This Jesus and This Power?

Trudy Sherry

> We often ask, "Why me?" and God replies, "It's not you, it is Me working through you." —*Anonymous*

"What? Why me?" Trudy sputtered. She was standing in the church courtyard drinking punch. "When Alice, Jane, and Bunnie came up to me, I didn't expect anything out of the ordinary."

They told her that God had "put your name on each of our hearts, and we believe *you* are to help us with the girls. We heard you tell about Jesus healing your son and about Him answering other prayers. We can see, Trudy, that you have a special relationship with the Lord.

"We're teaching sewing to thirty-five girls at a delinquent home. As we get to know the girls better, we tell them about Jesus. A few of them have asked Him to come into their lives. We'd like you to come to Kendall Hall and tell these girls how they can know Jesus like you know Him."

"The Lord is ingenious about how He plants His ideas in our minds," Trudy says. "God's will begins when a seed-thought is planted your mind. As you talk to the Lord about it, and let it rest awhile, you become assured that it's from Him. The secret of knowing if it's God's idea or the enemy's idea is the urgency-rush factor. God is never in a hurry; the enemy always wants us to hurry, panic, and do things without thinking them through. If an idea is from God, it grows quietly in your mind."

Trudy's main argument was, *But God, I've never been involved with teenagers. I'm a Brownie and Girl Scout leader. I know nothing about delinquent young people!*

"God waited patiently for me to finish spouting out all my arguments, and then He spoke quietly to me in my thoughts: *Obedience, Trudy.*"

"On our way home from the Lay Institute for evangelism, we prayed specifically what each of us should do," Jane and Bunnie told Trudy. "Now once a week we're teaching sewing to thirty-five girls living in cottages on a delinquent children's compound called Kendall Children's Home. As we get to know each of the girls better, we tell how much Jesus loves them and wants them to know Him. And one by one, girls have been asking Jesus to come into their lives. And now we'd like you, Trudy, to consider coming to Kendall with us."

"I need to pray about this," Trudy answered. "After I've heard from the Lord, I'll get back to you."

Trudy says, "I knew what He expected from me. I wanted to please Jesus, the One who had walked through so many difficult situations with me. I was willing to do anything He asked. *Yes, Lord, I will go*, I answered."

The first time Trudy drove onto the grounds of Kendall Children's Home, her first thoughts were, *How awful to be here!*

"There was a suggestion of loneliness from the various buildings spread so far apart," Trudy says. "And the look of coldness sent a chill through me. The layout of the buildings eliminated any feeling of coziness that the word *cottage* brings to mind. A feeling of solitary confinement struck me as I continued to drive through the ten-acre complex."

Once inside the building, Trudy found that the huge room where she was to speak had metal chairs set in two rows of semicircles. Women from the church were presenting an Easter program.

"As I sat at the back of the room, all I could see was thirty-five girls filled with hate and bitterness," Trudy says. "The girls seemed to be listening, but as I observed them closely, I saw that their attention wasn't on the story being told. They had put on a 'listening look'—one that so many teenagers are famous for: *Ho-hum. Here we go again. The same old stuff....* What they were hearing didn't mean anything to them. Why? Various ones had been involved in drugs, witchcraft, perversion, and even murder. Just about everything the Bible warns us against, these girls had already experienced.

"As I sat there, I didn't know what I was going to say. I waited, saying to myself, *Hurry up, Holy Spirit. Tell me, how I can reach this type of young people who have so many hurts.* The Bible verse from Luke 12:12 came to mind: The Holy Spirit will teach you at that time what you should say.

"After I had been introduced, I rose and walked to the front. Standing before the girls, all I saw was their hate and bitterness. *They are so different!* I thought.

"And that was the key—different. *I will tell them a different type of story!*

"Tell me," Trudy began, "suppose that after we finished here today, the administrator of Kendall came over and said, 'I would like to know if you would like to be an all-girls' basketball team. If you do, a bus will leave from here at 5 p.m. to take you to Killian High School. Once there, each of you will have a chance to play, then the game is over. Who do you think won the game?'

"One of the girls, speaking in a belligerent, sneering tone of voice, said, 'We got beat, of course.'

"You not only got beat; you got slaughtered! Why? Because unless you know the rules of the game and have played it together before, you can't play to win. And this is the same with God. He created you, but He didn't leave you without the rules. Neither did He leave you without a rule book to show you what the rules are and how to play in the game of life.

"You know what? God has changed my life! I know there is another way to live. I know that some of you girls are seventeen and you'll marry in a few years. And what are you going to tell your children? Will you tell them, 'Come on out here to Kendall Home. This is the way to live'? Of course, you know that isn't what you want to tell them. I've found in my life another way to live. And you don't have to live the way you are right now."

Now Trudy had the complete attention of every girl. "I knew what I had said had hit home."

She continued, "I want to tell you what has happened in *my* life. It's exciting! I want to tell you how very much God loves you and how He has a plan for each of you. If you really want to know why and how God loves you, the plan He has for *your* life, and about the power to live that plan, come here on Thursday and I'll introduce you to the Person who can show you. I don't want anyone to come because they think they have to. I want you to come because you want to find out."

"I think the girls were as dumbfounded as I was," Trudy says. "It was such a contrast—from a very religious story to a kind of crazy, unorthodox story."

Trudy continued to share with these girls for three years, and during that time hundreds of girls became Christians. "But," she says, "while there I came in contact with girls who had given their lives to Satan and were involved in occult worship. A large number of them were lesbians—a result of the need for being loved. Some had been raped; some were used by their fathers as wives; some had overdosed; some had been involved in murders.

"I had never come in contact with these horrible things before. Because I knew no one at that time to talk to about this, I turned to the Scriptures, depending entirely on the Holy Spirit for answers."

As Trudy continued her ministry at Kendall Home for three years, the girls told new girls coming in about the Jesus they had found, and many came to know Jesus!

More about Trudy Sherry:

Trudy's book, *Who Is This Jesus and This Power?* will come out sometime in the next year. The following is an excerpt from the book:

Two or three times Trudy cried out to God, "Oh, God, there has to be another way of life." Then she fell down on her knees.

"Suddenly the room began to light up with a brilliant light. To the left of me an image of a man—encircled by a brilliant light and dressed in a white robe—began to form. The light was so bright that I could hardly see. I knew nothing of the Bible. I didn't even have one in the house. I knew absolutely nothing about Jesus. I was awed; I wasn't even able to stand. I dropped to my knees."

Then Trudy saw two other figures to the right of this "man," and they also were dressed in white. "I was engulfed in a peace and love I had never experienced before. Tears began to stream down my cheeks. '*Who are You? What do You want?*' I whispered.

"Light now flooded the room, emanating from the first man in the brilliant white robe. He spoke in a gentle voice. *Now your life shall be lived for Me.*

"'*Who are You?*' I repeated. I felt an extreme love and peace that I'd never felt before. After that, the person spoke a very peaceful statement into my thoughts, then He was lifted up and went out the window up into the clouds. All I said to the other two men dressed in white was, '*Who is He and where is He going?*' I felt a love that penetrated my whole being."

Chapter 28

"Talk About Changed Lives!"

Beverly Castetter

When someone becomes a Christian he becomes a brand new person inside. He is not the same anymore. A new life has begun! (2 Corinthians 5:17 TLB).

"In my early childhood I went to church and Sunday school," Beverly says. "I knew the wonderful stories of the Bible well; still I had a deep hunger and thirst from not being able to relate these to my world—to the here and now. *What do these all have to do with me?* was my deep inner unrest."

Still in her late thirties, Beverly was married and had six children. "We were all in reasonably good condition according to worldly statistics," she says. "Then my world began to crumble.

"Our first daughter announced she was getting a divorce, and she came home bringing with her a young son. I agreed to take care of him so she could go back to college. About the same time, our fourth daughter was very involved with the young people's group at church. The pastor and the leader of the group had a disagreement, and she left the church. As you can imagine, all twenty-two young people also left. Sadly, the pastor did nothing to try to get them to return. I wasn't about to allow my daughter to drift away from church, so on Sundays my husband took the family and continued to attend church, while my daughter and I visited other churches.

"In the fall I joined a bowling league, feeling it would be an outlet for me and that my grandson would have kids his age to play with. The first day four girls walked in with LIVING WAY BIBLE BOOKSTORE written on the back of their shirts. My first thought was, *What are these crazy Christians doing here in the bowling alley?*

"Later I found out they had agreed to bowl and not talk about Jesus—unless asked. But talk about God being in control! They were good. So good they took every trophy for the year. How could anyone miss that? I believe they could have rolled a gutter ball and it would have bounced out of the gutter, and they would come away with a strike!

"There was always a crowd around them, and yes, they talked. After my recent experience I wouldn't let them get close. But I stayed on the sidelines and I listened.

"Trudy Sherry invited me to her house for a cup of coffee. The next day when I knocked on her door, she looked out her side window and saw me, but she didn't open the door. Rather, she talked to me *through* the window. 'Come on, Trudy,' I said. 'You invited me over for coffee, so open the door.'"

Trudy opened the door laughing and said, "That's like Jesus. He can't come in until you open the door of your life and invite Him in. You can know all about Him but not have Him in your life."

A light went on in Beverly's mind and she understood! She talked to Trudy about her concern over her daughter. Before she left, Trudy gave her *The Four Spiritual Laws* to share with her daughter.

"When I got home I tossed the booklet on the dresser," Beverly says. "And there it sat for three or four days. But every time I went past the dresser, my eyes were drawn to that booklet. It almost seemed as though the booklet was beckoning me to pick it up.

"Finally I had a few minutes alone, so I picked up the booklet, thinking I really should read it before I tried to share it with my daughter. I went out on the patio and devoured it completely.

"Then I thought, *Just in case I've missed something, maybe I ought to pray the prayer suggested here*. It felt so right, so good to pray. I prayed then immediately got up and dove into our swimming pool. A strange sensation came over me, and I felt that if I could stay underwater I would finally be clean. I stayed as long as I could, then when I finally surfaced I felt and saw a bright light—so bright I couldn't open my eyes. I flipped over on my back and felt a hand on my head and heard the words deep inside and knew I was being baptized.

"Needless to say, my life has never been the same, and neither have the lives of our children! Talk about changed lives! God has done a whale of a job in this family."

***More about Beverly Castetter*:**

Beverly and Laurel have been married sixty-three years, and their six children, one by one, have accepted Jesus Christ. They serve in the office of Calvary Chapel, Fort Lauderdale, Florida.

Chapter 29

"The Light of God's Word Flooded My Soul!"

Nell Jone M. Astudillo

I look up into the face of Jesus,
for there my heart can rest, my fears are stilled;
and there is joy, and love, and light for darkness,
and perfect peace and every hope fulfilled.
—*Anonymous, from the poem: "I Look Not Back"*

"My life began with martial arts. I loved martial arts, and I practiced hours every day," Nell says.

Yes, martial arts was Nell's god. At age sixteen when he started college in the Philippines, he became a karate champion in the national open black-belt tournament. During college he was at the top of everything he did. "I won all my tournaments in martial arts, was a model, an academic scholar in Mindanao Aeronautical Technical School, and an officer in ROTC. I had a lot of friends and girlfriends, and I liked to party!" he confesses.

"But I especially liked preparing for tournaments because the few days before the tournament was the only time I could be self-disciplined enough to stop drinking. On the outside I looked great—but I knew I was an alcoholic and a drug addict, and on the inside I was empty and filled with fear. One day during an earthquake I was so afraid I ran outside and knelt down and cried out to the Lord, 'Don't take me yet, Lord, I am still a sinner!' I was searching for truth, and sometimes I would even go to church after staying out and drinking all night with my buddies.

"I really wanted a stable life and I wanted to be good, true, and honest, but my life was a mess. One of my girlfriends and I even committed murder by killing our baby through an abortion.

"It all finally came to a head when the girlfriend I was with at the time told me she was leaving."

For three days Nell just sat on the beach, drinking, doing drugs, and smoking. "I kept thinking, *Why is life like this? I have everything the world has to offer—money and medals and honor and almost any woman I want, but my life is hopeless.* I even wondered if I should just commit suicide and end all the pain."

The third day Nell left the beach and wandered aimlessly through the mall asking, "God, why am I here? What do You want me to do? What is the purpose of life? Is the purpose of my life just to have fun, be rich, and play around with girls? Is there more to life than having power, money, and success?"

As these thoughts swirled through his head, a girl approached and asked if she could talk with him.

"Never one to turn down a beautiful gal, I stopped and listened to her. She told me about a Bible study and asked if I would be interested in attending. I wondered if this was the answer to my questions, so I thought I would try it out.

"We met in a restaurant and I remember the first question the leader asked was, 'Have you ever been in love?' I thought he was talking directly to me. 'What if you write a letter to someone you love,' he continued, 'and you're going to be gone for a long time. What will you write in it? Maybe you would write on nice stationery and seal it with a kiss, then give it to that special girlfriend.

"And it is a special letter because she loves you. But she just keeps it under her pillow or by her bed and never reads it. How would you feel? You would want to plead with her, 'I wrote all my love in that letter, please read it!'

"Someone wrote you a love letter and He wants to tell you how much He loves you. He has written the purpose of your life in this book."

He held up a Bible. "Have you read it?"

"I thought, *Oh, that's me! I have a Bible but I never read it. I don't even know what it says.*"

The Bible study leader continued, "God wrote a love letter to you."

"When he said those words, I knew I wanted to read that love letter. I instantly realized the Bible was the answer to all my questions and I wanted to know Jesus.

"I went home and read the Bible all night long. I didn't want to stop reading. It was as if my darkness was transformed as the light of God's Word flooded my soul. I used to do martial arts for hours every day. I would jog in the morning, train at the gym, and do martial arts every evening. I had built up my body, but I had not put time into my spirit, and I was so thirsty for more of God that I could hardly put my Bible down.

"I realized that I had no desire to drink even though I was an alcoholic. Friends came to my house and offered me beer, but I told them, 'I have something better than beer.'

"I had the Bible, and I had absolutely no desire to drink! Girls called, inviting me to parties. I would turn down their offers and begin sharing with them what I was reading in the Bible. I'd tell them how much they needed Jesus and how God could change their lives too.

"Of course, my old friends thought I was crazy because all I did was read my Bible, and I wouldn't even go out. I was so excited about the Bible I hardly left my room but just read and read. My old girlfriend called me up and I told her about Christ and that I had found Him and was so happy."

"You don't want me anymore?" she asked.

"I found God and He is all I want," Nell told her. "I want to serve the Lord Jesus. Life to me is now knowing Christ and serving God."

God led Nell to a church and gave him new friends—men who discipled him and helped him grow in Christ.

"For a number of years I had planned to join the Air Force, and right about that time I finally received the letter I had been waiting for saying I was accepted for training in Manila. I called my old girlfriend and she said it was great. But I struggled. I knew I could not grow in the Lord if I joined because I would have no time to read the Bible, and I would have no church to help me.

"My old girlfriend said if I didn't join the Air Force then it was over between us, and she told me would never talk with me again. I remembered that I had told her that I chose Christ over her. Did I really mean that?"

Nell prayed for two days asking, *God, what should I do? What is Your plan?* He opened the Bible and read the verse, *What good will it be for a man if he gains the whole world, yet forfeits his soul?* (Matthew 16:26). The next verse he read was Matthew 8:20, *The Son of Man has no place to lay his head.*

Besides martial arts, joining the military had been his life goal. "'God, if I drop this offer, I don't know where to go, and everything will have to be by faith.' But I knew what God was telling me to do, and I turned down the offer. My mom kicked me out of the house because I did not join the Air Force, so I moved into the church.

"The next major test was martial arts. I practiced or went to tournaments every night, but the church had ministry every night. I knew God had asked me to give up my girlfriend as well as the military. I realized the hardest part was giving up martial arts because it was my whole life. But I told God, '*If that is what You are calling me to do, I am even willing to give up martial arts!*'"

And Nell was true to his word. He dropped martial arts for a number of years. Then one day, he asked God to give him a job that paid the same as his current job but would give him more time in the Word.

"Right after that prayer," Nell says, "the gym hired me as a teacher for aerobics and kickboxing/tae bo. Then after a few years they asked me to start a martial arts program! So I started practicing martial arts again. The Lord restored to me what I had given up, but He also gave me so much more.

"God brought Cathy and her precious little girl, Tashaemae, into my life. Tashaemae is the same age as the child I would have had if my girlfriend had not had an abortion. How amazing is our God! He restored to me what my sin had destroyed in my life.

"Cathy and I married in April 2005. God not only gave me a beautiful wife and daughter but also a partner who works with me and helps me in so many areas. Cathy is very good with planning and helping me interact with people. Our daughter, Tashaemae, does martial arts and cheer dancing. She is now a second brown-belt in karate. She also helps me in my ministry, doing demonstrations.

"Cathy and I began counseling and ministering to kids with broken relationships. We share the gospel with them and tell them about Jesus. We also reach out to the parents, sharing with them about Christ.

"During that time God gave me a desire and a vision for a martial arts ministry. I began praying for someone to work with and that I could meet a martial arts ministry team. About three months later the American Bushido-Kai Karate Association came to the Philippines and did a demonstration at All Nations Christian Church. They are black belts in karate, and their goal is to share the gospel through martial arts. When I asked if I could be a part of their group, they said they had only one requirement: love for Christ and a desire to be used by Him.

"In 2008 I started King's Sword School of Martial Arts and Values. King's Sword stands for the Word of God from Ephesians 6:17. It is a twofold organization of martial arts and ministry. The purpose is to reach youth who do not have work, teach them quality martial arts, share the gospel with them, and help them find jobs.

"We go to churches, schools, villages, and youth gatherings, and do demonstrations and share the gospel. Many youth come to Jesus, and we always try to get them involved in a church. In the classes the students memorize warrior scriptures. We stress that 'the greatest self-defense is knowing the Word of God. It will not only save you physically but also for eternity.'

"My purpose in life now is so much more than martial arts. Martial arts is no longer my god, but simply a tool that God has restored to me to be used by the Lord to tell people about Jesus. I want to be like the apostle Paul who said, *For me to live is Christ and to die is gain* (Philippians 1:21).

"Jesus was the greatest warrior who ever lived. He is the Master of all martial arts. He is the Lord of lords and King of kings. The Bible says, *The LORD is a warrior; the LORD is his name* (Exodus 15:3).

"It is such an incredible blessing that I can practice and teach any type of martial arts and share His gift of salvation. God has given me the desires of my heart, all because the Light of God's Word flooded my soul!"

More about Nell Jone M Astudillo:

Nell has a second-degree black-belt karate in ABKA karate system and is a Certified Muay Thai Instructor. He is the chief instructor in ABKA-Philippines and founder of King's Sword Martial Arts.

Chapter 30

"Lord, I Need Help!"

David Hatcher

Meditate in God's light; glow in the darkness of trial.
—*Dr. Erwin Lutzer*

"Lord, I need help! I'm trying to keep my sanity. These ropes have cut my arms. We've been beaten, marched through the streets, spit on, and deprived of sleep. I've got boils on my body. I'm sick with flu. I've prayed all the prayers I know. I've quoted all the Scripture I can remember—but still no relief. Help me, Father God! I don't think I can make it through another day of suffering. I feel I need to have some sign from You—a sign that will tell me that You will help me!"

That desperate plea came from David Hatcher as he languished in a cold, dark prison cell. His ankles were in leg irons, and manacles held his wrists and forearms so tightly together that his chest bled. His body ached with pain. His heart was dark with hatred for his captors.

In May 30, 1966, only two weeks remained in his tour of duty in Vietnam as an Air Force pilot. "I was a fighter pilot," David says. "I flew a single-seat fighter/bomber called the F-105 Thunderchief. This supersonic plane could carry bombs of different sizes—

including an atomic bomb as well as rockets, missiles, and a gatling gun that could shoot 300 rounds per second of twenty-millimeter shells. It was my job to kill and destroy the enemy. And I was good at my job. I had made several flights across the Atlantic with the aid of in-flight refueling, and one trip across the Pacific in this single-seat F-105."

David was leading a flight of four of those F1-05s loaded with bombs deep into North Vietnam territory. Their mission was to destroy a bridge some twenty miles southwest of Hanoi. It was the eighty-seventh mission into North Vietnam toward a 100-mission tour of duty. Some twenty minutes away from the target, David thought about the crude life and disposition of a fighter pilot—confident, cocky, proud, fearless. As he thought of returning to his family and being a husband to his wife and father to his young daughters, he mouthed a silent prayer: *Help me, Lord, to get my act together before I return to my family. Do a deeper spiritual work in my life. You know it's only two more weeks!*

But that was not to be. Those two weeks turned into seven long years.

Thirty minutes after that prayer, David's plane was hit by anti-aircraft fire, and he was floating into the jungle in a parachute. He evaded the enemy the rest of that day and night and then was captured. Seven long years of mental, physical, and spiritual torture as a prisoner of war followed.

From May 31 through early October, "Mr. Tough Guy," David says, "was near the breaking point."

It was just four months and one week later, on the night of October 6, 1966,[1] that David cried out to the Lord asking for "a sign that will tell me that You will help me endure!"

David says, "To say the least, I did not like the Vietnamese! The prison guards were out to break me. Despite my hatred of them, I forgave those guards—and the others—the rest of the years remaining in the infamous Hanoi Hilton.[2] I gained strength and resolve to resist and press on. God was working to make me into a new creation!"

David had spent a sleepless night, and now the sun was rising as he finished his plea for a sign. Right at that moment, a shaft of sunlight beamed through a nail hole in his cell door. Suddenly the back wall of his cramped cell lit up with a heavenly light!

"When that shaft of sunlight hit the wall, the presence of God filled my whole cell. The Lord heard my prayer and gave me the sign I felt I needed. Then I knew beyond a shadow of doubt that He would help me make it!" The Lord gave David a poem as he lay there shackled, and He wrote it in his memory:

Good morning, Lord, I'm feeling fine
And thanks to You, I'm doing okay.

Thank You, Lord, for a night of rest.
Thank You for sweet blessedness.
Thank You for your love divine.
And for my peace of mind.

Forgive me, Lord, for sins I've done.
Forgive me for the men I've wronged.
Teach me to forgive my foe
And those who wish me harm.

Now go with me this day today.
Help me to resist and say,
"I love my Lord and I love my land
And I'll praise Your name as long as I can!"

"From that day forward, whenever I was in a bind or needed supernatural help, I shouted, 'Good morning, Lord, I'm feeling fine…'

"Yes, that prayer given me by the Lord of Light sustained me for the rest of my captivity. And after I was released, the Lord whispered in my ear, *The words of that poem still have the same power. You should use it more often.* And I replied, 'Yes, Lord, I hear You loud and clear!'

"So today when things get rough in my life—and I've learned that Satan will see to it that we all face rough times when we seek to follow the Lord—I repeat that poem."

God's light dispelled that dark shadow of doubt! And David did endure and returned home to his wife and children. Today David says, "I prayed, *Lord, do a deeper spiritual work in my life!* He answered that prayer by my experience of confinement in a stinking cell in the Hanoi Hilton."

***More about David Hatcher*:**

David and Willie had been married eleven years when he left for Vietnam. They had attended the same small high school. David graduated in 1952, and Willie graduated in 1953. In May 1955, Willie rode the train for three days to meet David in Harlingen, Texas. There, all on the same day—May 9th—David finished flying school and received his "wings," a 2nd-lieutenant bars, and his wife!

Their oldest daughter, Liz, was born on August 2, 1961; Alison came next on September 17, 1962, while they were stationed in West Germany. Liz and Alison were only three and four years old when David left from Goldsboro, North Carolina, to go to Vietnam.

When Willodene heard news of David's capture, she responded with determination and perseverance. Not knowing for sure she would ever see David alive again, she took a step of faith: through the years of waiting, she set out to build a new house for David to return to. One of their little daughters responded with faith as well, and brought her mom the entire contents of her piggy bank—a grand total of $2.52!

David says of Willie: "She was a real trouper in raising our two cute daughters." David and Willie have been blessed with five grandchildren: Liz has a daughter in the teaching fellows program at Boone and a son at North Carolina State. Alison has three boys, ages nine, eleven, and thirteen. All three are ball players. And Granddad and Grandmom like to watch them play ball!

1 In an e-mail from David on October 21, 2011, David wrote: "I just realized that I defeated Satan on his day October 6, '66—666. God is good! Also the Lord gave me another daily prayer last night: *And they overcame him because of the blood of the Lamb and because of the word of their testimony, and they did not love their life even to death!* (Revelation 12:11).

2 Hoa Lo Prison, later sarcastically known to American prisoners of war as the "Hanoi Hilton" or "Heartbreak Hotel," was a prison used by the French colonists in Vietnam for political prisoners and later by North Vietnam for prisoners of war during the Vietnam War. The name *Hoa Lo*, commonly translated as "fiery furnace" or even "hell's hole," also means "stove." The name originated from the street name, where many stores along the street sold woodstoves and coal-fire stoves.

Chapter 31

Creativity and Faith—God's Gifts

Louise Bass

"See, I have chosen Bezalel...[and Louise] and I have filled [them] with the Spirit of God, with skill, ability and knowledge...to make artistic designs..." (Exodus 31:2–4).

Those two words—*creativity* and *faith*—describe Louse Bass perfectly. Both are gifts from God. Just as Bezalel was "chosen" and "filled with the Spirit of God," so God has chosen Louise and filled her with His Holy Spirit.

"Because God created me to create and serve Him in a special way," Louise says, "I find fulfillment as I use my talent as an artist."

Louise is indeed a talented artist,[1] but when I think of her, I first think of her as a woman of great faith—even as I think of George Mueller of a man of great faith![2]

As she says, God created her to create. But we might ask ourselves, *Did He create us to have faith?*

Certainly we can say that His desire for each of us is that we place our faith in His Son, Jesus. But we were born without that faith; we were born as sinners. And those whose parents have placed their faith in Jesus—as Louise's parents had—are blessed.

Louise is one of those blessed ones. She placed her faith in Jesus at an early age.

When Jack, her husband, died in 1979, Louise accepted this as God's will and rejoiced to think of him being in God's presence praising Him—"the one thing above all others that he had loved doing," she says.

Yes, Jack died. And recently their son died. She grieved, but at the same time rejoiced that he was free of all suffering. She never blamed God, never questioned Him.

More about Louise Bass:

Louise Bass lives in the suburbs of Traverse City, Michigan. When Louise was a child, her parents told her Bible stories. They also read the Bible and other books to her. A few years ago Bible Translation and Literacy (BTL), a Wycliffe Affiliate Organization (WAO), in Kenya, needed an artist to illustrate reading books and Scripture portions for new literates. BTL is one of around two dozen WAOs in various countries around the world. You may contact BTL at BTL@sil.org or PO Box 44456, Nairobi, Kenya. For many years Louise had drunk deeply from God's Word, so her ears were attuned to the Holy Spirit's prompting regarding BTL's need. She went to Kenya and volunteered her expertise.

A few years ago, as a volunteer artist with the Reformed Church of America, she illustrated the book *Light from Tzeltal Lamps*, devotions from pastors, translated and compiled by Sam and Helen Hofman.

Currently Louise is finalizing a book with a working title of *Sketches of a Bible Illustrator* about her experience with the Holy Spirit when in Papua New Guinea. She hopes to see it published this year. You may email Louise at LBasspond@gmail.com to request a copy.

Sitting before her fireplace in Michigan, Louise praises God for His gift that enables her to express His Word visually. "Some who will not read the words of Scripture respond to a visual expression of the Word of God," she says.

1 Louise and her husband, Jack, spent twenty years in Papua New Guinea (PNG). There in PNG Louise used her gift of creativity by illustrating books for translators. When home for a furlough in 1979, Jack came back from running and entered their garage, and right then the Lord took Jack to be with Him. Louise then used her artistic talent to work commercially to earn money for seeing her children through their schooling.

2 Jack and Louise were our friends when we were in PNG, and we have remained friends with Louise even though she lives in Michigan and we live in North Carolina.

Chapter 32

Lost

Ben Proffit

I remember the fear that filled me when as a small child. I wandered out of our yard and couldn't find my way back home. I was lost! But my father came looking for me and he found me. That fear was nothing compared to the fear that gripped me when I grew up and discovered I was lost eternally. And this time my heavenly Father came looking for me. And He found me! —*Allen Loring*

"It was the darkest night I have ever seen, literally so black I couldn't see my hand in front of my face," Ben says.

On that "darkest night" that Ben had ever seen, he was lost in the "jungle" in the Smokey Mountains National Park in Tennessee. Not only was the night black, a cold wind had started blowing, and a hard rain began, causing the temperature to fall rapidly.

It was October 1991, and Ben's job in a family crisis intervention center required him to attend a training retreat in Tennessee. There he and a long-lost buddy from seminary days in Louisiana met once again. "Jerry and I had been good friends and weekly partners in sharing Christ around the Bourbon Street area of New Orleans," Ben says.

"For the first two days of the retreat, rain poured down without slacking. But still Jerry and I had not found time to catch up on each other's news. So we pledged that after supper of our final night, we would grab rockers and talk and gaze at the mountain peak. But when the rain finally stopped, I told Jerry that I couldn't spend three days within fifty feet of the park without walking at least one trail. I suggested we visit when I returned."

Ben's friend suggested a trail called "The Old Settlers Road" and gave him a simple hand-drawn map. "That road runs along a creek in the big trees. Watch for a turn in about a mile that will take you back here," he said.

"The weather was warm and glorious, so I put on a short-sleeved shirt and tied a thin cotton jacket around my waist. I had barely begun when I found a cemetery filled with markers that were all a hundred fifty to two hundred years old. Next I passed numerous large stone walls, which pioneers probably built as they cleared fields for planting and simply stacked rocks out of their way.

"Then I passed a few huge stone chimneys and sites of original cabins. One cabin even had a few logs still in place. Suddenly the whole place became mystical to me as it occurred to me that my ancestor, Ben, may have walked this exact road. *Perhaps one of these sites was his home*, I thought. I was elated as I saw the historic significance and enthralled by the natural beauty all around me."

Just past an overgrown firebreak, Ben saw a national park sign that indicated the trail direction. "So," he says, "I trekked on—but soon, between the steep mountains, thick forest canopy, and heavy clouds, it seemed that daylight was all but gone.

"My focus turned to getting out of the forest. *But,* I thought, *I don't have time to backtrack.* I was certain that I had not missed a trail intersection. So I walked faster and kept looking for a sign of a trail. *Surely,* I reasoned with myself, *even if I've missed a turn, this trail will ultimately come out somewhere in civilization.*

"The darker it got, the faster I walked, till eventually I was running. Just as it got too dark to see, the trail ended at a roaring creek, which I thought was a waterfall. As I stood there in the dark, with a cold wind blowing and the rain pelting down, reality set in. I knew I would not get back to the retreat center that night! And I knew I was in serious trouble.

"Prayer was part of the purpose of this trek, so I had already been in earnest discussion with God for some time. Now my prayers shifted to pleas for wisdom and guidance for what I should do.

"I needed shelter from the rain and wind. I tried to twist off evergreen limbs, but every tree was too limber for me to do so. I tried to burrow in leaves, but everything was so wet that it was pointless. I was near one of those massive chimneys, so I dug away enough debris to crawl inside and stick my head up the flue. But water was running down on my shoulders, and I knew I would freeze before daylight.

"Again my prayers shifted—this time I prayed for survival! And I believe it was God's Spirit who prompted me to get up and keep moving in order to circulate my blood and warm my muscles.

"I decided to walk back in the direction I had come from. Within minutes I wandered off the trail and into the ridges. Trying to see was pointless, so after a limb caught my face, I put my glasses in my pocket, closed my eyes, held my hands out in front, and started taking baby steps. It seemed like I was feeling for a doorway while trying not to fall down a stairway. With no way to know what was coming next, every step took extra focus, and still I repeatedly tripped, fell, and tumbled on rocks and into trees. My body was covered in cuts and bruises, and I began to wonder when the next step might be my last.

"Finally it happened—I stepped into thin air! It happened so suddenly that I couldn't even reach for tree branches. I slid feet-first downward about one hundred feet and landed in water just deep enough to absorb some of the fall before the rocks punched the breath out of me. My first thought was how much that hurt, and second was, *If my legs are broken, I'm as good as dead.* Ironically, lying in the mountain water was actually warmer than standing in the cold wind. So I lay there a few minutes trying to think what to do next. Then, I moved one limb at a time—each leg and each arm—and the results were good! I was able to stand up and walk. I was beat up and tired, so I crawled to the edge of a rock, face out of the water and collapsed asleep for a few minutes, until the terrible cold shivered me back awake.

"The water was so high and roaring that I was sure I was just above a waterfall. I crawled all along the bank and found only rock walls. I crossed the creek and felt only rock walls along that bank as well. It seemed that I was trapped in a canyon, so I had no choice but to crawl downstream, trying to stay feet-first and praying to feel a rock below me before letting go of any hold above me. I found dirt on one bank and was able to pull myself up using tree roots and limbs. Again I was so exhausted when I reached a flat spot up the ridge that I lay down awhile. But even exhaustion did not allow me to sleep in such cold.

"I realized the seriousness of my situation and tried to pass the time and muster courage by praying, singing, and quoting Scripture. Hour after hour, I prayed for every person and every need that came to mind. I quoted every Bible passage, even partial verses that I could remember, and I sang at the top of my voice every hymn and every song I remembered. Some of that loudness was meant to keep bears away from me! My theme for the night became, *Yea though I walk through the valley of the shadow of death, I will fear no evil, for Thou art with me.* I repeated that passage between almost every other meditation, and I considered each word as an entire prayer focus in itself."

So Ben kept walking and walking. His pace got slower and slower, and his body became colder and colder, and he grew more exhausted with each step. "Intentionally shivering hard helped," he says, "but then I became dizzy. My feet and legs would lock up and go rigid and cause almost unbearable pain. Every few steps I lay down and rubbed my feet, forcing the muscles to loosen so I could walk again. The wind began to blow harder, and it seemed to grow colder by the minute. I knew the danger of hypothermia and tried desperately to keep moving—and to keep praying. I remembered my army days when we were taught to make our bodies do more than what feels like the breaking point."

An obsessive thought drove Ben onward: *My kids cannot grow up without a father.* Ben's father, a pastor, had died when he was two years old. Ben says, "I believe the most negative shaping influence of my early life was the lack of a father, and I pleaded with God to not let my kids become fatherless.

"When I felt I just couldn't go on, I'd shout, 'Just one more step, one more step, one more....' The cramping became so bad that I had to lie down and rub my feet after every three to four steps. The cold became more than I felt I could take. Then the last straw—I found that I wandered into a thicket of underbrush. I ran into tree limbs at every height, in every direction. I was so cold and exhausted that I sat down and admitted, *I can't take one more step.* I cried out to God, '*There's no one here but You and me. I've nothing to hide, nothing to pretend. What must I do to prepare to meet You?*'

"It was almost as though an audible voice spoke to me, '*Praise Me to your last breath.*'

"I thought I had already prayed everything I knew how to pray, sang every song I knew. But spontaneously I began singing words that came from a memory I didn't know I had.

"*O soul, are you weary and troubled, no light in the darkness you see?* Those words struck me as so funny that I rolled on the ground belly-laughing. Then I sang again, *There's light for a look at the Savior and life more abundant and free. Turn your eyes upon Jesus.*

Look full in His wonderful face, and the things of earth will grow strangely dim, in the light of His glory and grace (taken from the hymn "Turn Your Eyes Upon Jesus").

"Such unconditional, sweet surrender into the arms of my Savior! I had never known such perfect peace. The holy presence of the Living God completely overwhelmed me, and joy flooded my soul as I wept in worship to God.

"I thought, *I'm ready to meet God.* And I expected to lie back, go unconscious, and quietly die. But while sitting there awestruck by the nearness of God, I looked up and saw a young man about twenty feet in front of me. He was wearing hiking clothes—but everything about him was white and glowing. He faced me for only a moment, then he turned halfway and made a 'Come follow me' motion with one arm. Next he took one step away from me. His second step curved upward, and his third was straight up and out of sight. He had been visible for perhaps ten seconds.

"I was stunned. My mind had trouble accepting what I had seen. I felt as though I was watching myself from the treetops. *This will be the moment my spirit will leave my body and follow that angel to heaven,* I thought. I sat waiting for several minutes and nothing happened. *Maybe the angel's motion meant I should stand up and walk in that 'follow me' direction.*"

So Ben stood up. "Suddenly I realized that I was not cold and my legs were not cramped. I was neither exhausted nor dizzy. My renewed energy astonished me! I walked in the direction the angel had indicated and exited the thicket without touching even one limb. The slope down the ridge seemed to me like a wide-open road covered with leaves. At the valley bottom, as I intersected a shallow creek, I felt a change in the ground. I was positive that I was on a hard-packed dirt trail. I got down on my knees and crawled along. The path led toward the creek, but the ground on the opposite bank was too soft and muddy to tell whether or not the path continued there."

Ben decided to follow the path in the opposite direction. "*It must be near dawn by now*, I thought, *so I'll keep walking back and forth on this dirt area till daylight. I will not lose this trail.* As I took my first step, I thought I saw a firefly flickering up ahead and I stopped to watch it. Then I realized it was too cold for fireflies. *But what can it be?* I squatted down and stared hard. The light was moving steadily across a ridgeline. I began to run toward it, breaking through brush shouting.

"Then I thought, *Maybe I ought to stay in place as long as it doesn't move out of my sight.* At about one hundred yards it turned straight toward me, and I knew it was a flashlight.

"I yelled out, 'Hey, Jerry, is that you?' and then the light jerked upward about two feet. It was a park ranger, and I'd about scared the life out of him."

"Ben, is that you?" the ranger yelled back to Ben.

"I stood in place and thanked God to be found alive," Ben says.

The park ranger gave Ben a warm coat, water, and a candy bar. "Will you need a stretcher?" he asked, and Ben assured him that though he was tired, he was sure that he could walk out. Then the park ranger radioed other rangers, and they made plans to meet. He gave Ben a flashlight and instructed him to follow him.

"We took turns shining our flashlights for each other to rock-climb down one cascade after another," Ben says. "It was hard and the ranger had to help me find footing several times. Suddenly we broke into open sky, and there was the highway and two rangers in a Jeep. They handed me a cup of coffee and laughed as I hugged the cup against my face to feel the warmth."

Driving back to the center, the rangers told Ben of their search tactic. Three men had walked in three different directions. They all guessed that he had traveled an opposite trail, so they concentrated on seventeen miles from where they found Ben. The ranger who found Ben said he was going through the motions of covering the five miles from where he had started, and he had misread his map and overshot his exit creek by a mile. Nobody had been assigned to look where Ben was found.

As Ben thanked them, one of them said, "You're lucky it wasn't a couple of degrees colder. Hypothermia could have been a big problem for you."

Of course, Ben knew that it was not luck that had caused them to find him—and he thanked God that He had been the One in charge.

"When Christians speak of 'lost' people, a strong image of their predicament now fills my mind," Ben says.

***More about Ben Proffit*:**

Ben and Malinda grew up 100 yards from each other through the woods and married after high school days. They have two girls and two boys, and are expecting their third grandchild.

Ben works as director of missions of one hundred and eight Southern Baptist Churches.

Ben's mother, growing up in a log cabin on the Nolichucky River, listened to her Uncle Joe talk about his experience in the Civil War, and her dad told combat stories from the Spanish-American War. But most intriguing to Ben were the stories from his dad's family, especially of Ben Proffit. In 1795 this ancestor of Ben's built a log raft, strapped a rifle and an axe on his back, and floated the French Broad River from North Carolina through the mountains to disembark on land that would soon become the state of Tennessee. The "Old Ben" was a Revolutionary War veteran and apparently a rugged and resourceful man.

"Malinda and I grew up as neighbors, so we have been close since diaper days. As teenagers we became inseparable, best friends, and we married right after high school, thirty-eight years ago. We have four grown children: Rebecca, Sarah, Seth, and Nathan, two wonderful sons-in-law, Jacob and Leo, and three precious granddaughters, Dora, Maomi, and Greta.

"My early years were consumed by alcohol and drugs, until I was twenty years old. At that time Christ completely transformed my life. To leave the old life behind, I enlisted in the army and served as a chaplain's assistant. Following God's call to that ministry, my education has included a BA in psychology from the University of South Carolina at Aiken and a master's in religious education from New Orleans Baptist Theological Seminary.

"In 1989, we left a thriving full-time church in Statesboro, Georgia, to become intentionally bi-vocational in Johnson City, Tennessee, so we could help establish a mission church. I earned a living by working 'intensive in-home family crisis intervention' for eleven years. When the mission church was strong and thriving, I volunteered to lead strategy planning and develop smaller churches throughout the 100-plus churches of Holston Baptist Association. Soon I began what is now seventeen years on staff, five of which were as a bi-vocational 'smaller church development specialist,' eleven years as full-time associate director, one year as interim DOM, and now one year as director of missions.

"The year 2009 marked another great turning point in my life. A motorcycle wreck and heart attack within four months left me broken, shattered, and torn from head to toe. The former nimble athlete and tireless worker is now weak and slow, and long months of brokenness and crying out to God allowed the Potter to remold His clay and teach prayerful dependence. I should have died four times, and ten surgeries later, my sovereign Papa-God has given me ears to hear and eyes to see. I am born for such a time as this, and God has gone out of His way to keep me alive for this moment in history. My mantra is, 'How dare we pray for anything less than spiritual awakening in us and a mighty movement of God through us—O God, whatever it takes!'"

Chapter 33

"It Was As If God Had Removed My Eyes and Replaced Them with His"

K. P. Yohannan

"I am sending you to open their eyes and turn them from darkness to light, and from the power of Satan to God, so that they may receive forgiveness of sins, and a place among those who are sanctified by faith in me" (Acts 26:17–18).

"O God, let one of my boys preach!"

Achyamma's eyes stung with salty tears. But those tears were not from the cooking fire or the hot spices that wafted up from the pan. She realized time was short. Her six sons were growing beyond her influence, yet not one showed any sign of going into the gospel ministry.

Except for the youngest—little "Yohannachan," as he was known—every one of her children seemed destined for secular work.

And so it was that Achyamma prayed in despair, "O God, let just one of my boys preach."

Like Hannah and so many other saintly mothers in the Bible, little Yohannachan's mother had dedicated her children to the

Lord. That morning while preparing breakfast, she vowed to fast secretly until God called one of her sons into His service. Every Friday for the next three and a half years, she fasted. Her prayer was always the same. But nothing happened.

"Finally, only I, scrawny and little—the baby of the family—was left. There seemed little chance that I would preach. Although I had stood up in an evangelistic meeting at age eight, I was shy and timid and kept my faith mostly to myself. I showed no leadership skills and avoided sports and school functions. I was comfortable on the edge of village and family life, a shadowy figure who moved in and out of the scene almost unnoticed," K. P.[1] says.

"Then when I was sixteen, my mother's prayers were answered. A visiting gospel team from Operation Mobilization came to our church to present the challenge of faraway North India. My ninety-pound frame strained to hear every word as people on the team spoke and showed slides of the north."

They told of stonings and beatings they had received while preaching in non-Christian villages of North India, far from K. P.'s home in South India.

As the gospel team portrayed the desperately lost condition of people in 500,000 villages without a gospel witness, "I felt a strange sorrow for the lost," K. P. says. "That day I vowed to help bring the Good News of Jesus Christ to those strange and mysterious states to the north. My decision to go into the ministry largely resulted from my mother's faithful prayers. When I announced my decision, she handed me twenty-five rupees—enough for my train ticket. I set off to apply to the mission's headquarters."

And there K. P. got his first rebuff. Because he was underage, at first the mission's directors refused to let him join the teams going north. But he was permitted to attend the annual training conference. There he met missionary spokesman George Verwer, who challenged K. P. as never before to commit himself to a life of breathtaking, radical discipleship.

"That night in bed, I argued with both God and my own conscience. By two o'clock in the morning, my pillow was wet with sweat and tears. I shook with fear. *What if God asked me to preach in the streets? How would I ever be able to stand up in public and speak? What if I were stoned and beaten?*

"I knew myself all too well. I could hardly bear to look a friend in the eye during a conversation, let alone speak to hostile crowds on behalf of God. I realized I was behaving like Moses behaved when God called him."

Suddenly K. P. felt that he was not alone in the room. "A great sense of love and of being loved filled the place. I felt the presence of God and fell on my knees beside my bed. *Lord God,* I gasped in surrender to His presence and will, *I'll give myself to speak for You—but help me to know that You are with me.*

"In the morning, I awoke to a world and people suddenly different. As I walked outside, the Indian street scenes looked the same as before: children ran between the legs of people; cows, pigs, and chickens wandered about; vendors carried baskets of bright fruit and flowers on their heads. But I loved them all with a supernatural, unconditional love I'd never felt before. It was as if God had removed my eyes and replaced them with His eyes so I could see people as the heavenly Father sees them—lost and needy but with potential to glorify and reflect Him.

"I walked to the bus station with my eyes filled with tears of love. I knew that these people were all going to hell—and I knew God did not want them to go there. I had such a burden for these masses that I had to stop and lean against a wall just to keep my balance. I knew I was feeling the burden of love that God feels for the lost multitudes of India. His loving heart was pounding within mine, and I could hardly breathe. I paced back and forth to keep my knees from knocking in fright.

"'Lord,' I cried out, 'If You want me to do something, tell me and give me courage.'"

Then looking up, K. P. saw a huge stone. He immediately knew he had to climb up on that stone and preach to the crowds. "I felt a force," he says, "like ten thousand volts of electricity shooting through my body.

"I began by singing a simple children's chorus. By the time I finished, a crowd stood at the foot of the rock. I had not prepared myself to speak, but God took over and filled my mouth with words of His love. I preached the gospel to the poor as Jesus commanded His disciples to do. As the power and authority of God flowed through me, I had supernatural boldness."

Others from the Operation Mobilization Gospel teams stopped to listen. That was in 1966, and K. P. says, "The question of my age and calling never came up again."

After serving with Operation Mobilization for nearly eight years on the Indian subcontinent, K. P. felt the need to take time to study further and seek God's face for his future ministry. God, in His providence, directed his path to the United States, to attend seminary at Criswell College in Dallas, Texas. While in college, K. P. married Gisela, a missionary from Germany who had served the Lord together with him in India.

After K. P.'s ordination, he was called for a season to pastor a local church in the Dallas area. But his heart ached for the lost millions in India and neighboring countries, and with the passage of time, he began to lack peace about continuing to pastor in America. After seeking the Lord, he resigned his pastorate and started the mission now known as Gospel for Asia.

K. P. and Gisela moved to a tiny town in Oklahoma where a pastor friend had offered some free office space for their first mission headquarters. That was 1979. Today, GFA sends out thousands of national missionaries from many Asian countries to take the gospel to those who have never heard.

But the growth did not happen without trial and suffering. At the beginning, nobody knew the name K. P. Yohannan or Gospel for Asia. K. P. recalls, "The Oklahoma days were characterized by periods of the most painful waiting I had ever faced. We were alone in a strange land, utterly at the end of our own strength, and desperately dependent upon God."

But the Lord was always faithful. The following incident demonstrates God's marvelous intervention in a situation that seemed absolutely hopeless.

In the early days, speaking engagements were hard for K. P. to come by, but that was the only way he knew for GFA to grow. After many weeks of calling, writing, and waiting, K. P. was finally ready in the winter of 1980 for his first major speaking tour. He purchased a budget airline ticket that gave him unlimited travel for twenty-one days. During those twenty-one days, he had appointments in eighteen cities throughout the Southwest, from Dallas to California.

"On the day of my departure, a terrible winter storm hit the region. All buses—including the one I planned to take from Oklahoma to Dallas—were cancelled. Our old Nova had some engine problems, so a neighbor offered to let me use an old pickup without a heater. The vehicle looked as if it could not make it to the next town. But it was either the pickup or nothing. If I missed my flight out of Dallas, my tightly packed schedule would be ruined. I had to go now!"

K. P. put on two pairs of socks and all the clothing he could. But even with the extra protection, after only a few minutes of driving, "it appeared I had made a terrible mistake," K. P. says. "A freezing snow covered the windshield in minutes. After every mile I had to stop, get out, and scrape the windows again. Soon my feet and gloves were soaked and frozen. I realized that the journey was going to take a lot longer than the six hours that were left before my flight. In my worst scenario, I saw the headlines reading, 'Preacher Freezes to Death in Winter Storm.' My head dropped to the steering wheel and I cried out to God....

"Then as I looked up, I saw a miracle on the windshield. The ice was melting rapidly before my eyes. Warmth flooded the truck. I looked at the heater, but nothing was coming out. The storm continued to rage all the way to Dallas, but inside the truck it was always warm, and the windshield was always clear."

K. P. made his flight, and the Lord gave him favor in the eyes of everyone he met during the tour. Then, after his last engagement in California on the last day of the tour, K. P. recalls that "a man came up and said that God had told him to donate his second car to me. So I cancelled my airline reservation and drove all the way home, rejoicing in the car God had provided!"[2]

More about K. P Yohannan:

Dr. K. P. Yohannan is the founder and international director of Gospel for Asia (GFA). He is the author of more than 200 books and is also an internationally known speaker and missionary statesman. He has traveled millions of miles to speak on behalf of the suffering and needy in our world. He and Gisela have two grown children, Daniel and Sarah, who both serve the Lord with their families. You may find out more about GFA's ministry by going to www.gfa.org or emailing them at info@gfa.org or by telephoning 1-800-2742.

1 Over the years, it has become easier for people to refer to K. P. Yohannan by his initials "K. P." than by his full name.

2 The information in this chapter on the life and work of K.P. Yohannan was taken from his book, *Revolution in World Missions*. To learn more about Gospel for Asia and order a free copy of this book, visit www.gfa.org. Or you may call the GFA office nearest you:

Australia 1300-889-339
Canada 1-888-WIN-ASIA
Germany 07623-79-74-77
New Zealand 0508-918-918
South Africa 041-360-0198
South Korea 080-801-0191
United Kingdom 09104-643-233
United States 1-800-WIN-ASIA

Appendix A: Books on Light and Miracles

These brochures may be ordered from Livingwaters.com or you may phone 1-800-437-1893 and order. They are not copyrighted so a person can make copies of them.

A Fax from Heaven, Faye Aldridge
A Light for Our Path, Jerry and Jan Allen
Christian Miracles: Amazing Stories of God's Helping Hand in our Everyday Lives, James S. Bell and Stephen R. Clark
George Mueller: Man of Faith and Miracles, Basil Miller
Miracles Are for Real: What Happens When Heaven Touches Earth, James L. Garlow and Keith Wall
Miracles Still Happen: Inspiring Real-Life Stories of Supernatural Intervention, Sheri Stone and Therese Marszalek
The Healing Code, Dr. Alex Loyd and Dr. Ben Johnson

Appendix B: Resources on Salvation

"Are You a Good Person?" brochure
In case you would like to talk to Dean Jordan or Jim Hollister about using the "Good Person" survey, e-mail Dean_Jordan@sil.org or Jim_Hollister@jaars.org and one of them will respond as soon as possible.

Four Spiritual Laws
God's Invitation: His Plan and His Purpose, Disciples International
disciplesinternational@verizon.net